"This book is 100 percent engaging. Dave Roche has managed to bring humor and humanity and, dare I say, a human face to a deeply personal and often challenging story. This man is clearly neither victim nor hero, but rather a beautifully complicated creature, like each and every one of us."

—Tracey Friesen, Executive Producer, Pacific and Yukon Centre National Film Board of Canada, Producer of Shameless: The ART of Disability

"...d is very funny, but this book made me weep. I did not cry with ... but because of this man's courage and grace. This book is about ... of self-discovery and a disfigured man's belief in human beings ... own great heart."

—... L. Mason, President and CEO, Girl Scouts of Colorado, 2007

"...r and grace, David Roche shares his philosophy of life, love ...y. He learned late in life that his disfigured face is a gift and ...hers to see, and understand, themselves. The Church of ... a brief, humorous and profound guide to life for each ...us."

—...n E. Brown, author of Movie Stars and Sensuous Scars

"...t life should come with an instruction manual. Now ...tten one—chock full of hilarious wisdom."

—...rsimmon Blackbridge, artist, writer and performer

"...everent book, wise, very funny, uplifting, filled ...t love. A wonderful story of the growth and tri- ...'s personal physician and friend, I have been a ...n his remarkable journey. I couldn't put the ...iately reread it."

—Ken Barnes, M.D.

"...ur-face narrative of his journey to self- ...real substance inviting the reader to dig

...d Executive Director, AboutFace USA

"I normally balk at using the superlative 'inspirational' to describe the work of artists with disabilities. But this book, like his performance work, is inspirational in the best sense. Never cloying or unduly sentimental, Roche shares with us complex lessons learned from navigating life with a conspicuous face. As a cultural outsider/insider, Roche has developed a keen sense of observation and a warm, engaging wit that magnetizes his audiences. Roche is always a lover of humanity, and finds beauty and grace in the most unlikely places. And he's just damn funny."

—*Carrie Sandahl, Associate Professor,*
School of Theatre, Florida State University

"David Roche now takes his rightful place somewhere between Mark Twain and the Dalai Lama; between Harpo Marx and Mother Teresa. His Church of 80% Sincerity might start as a joke, but the punch line is nothing less than a vision of the 'beloved community.' A master storyteller, David nudges us into the realization that we are all disfigured. He mirrors all our hidden wounds and leads us, laughing all the way, toward the possibility of healing."

—*Corey Fischer, Founding Member, Traveling Jewish Theatre*

"With his generosity of heart, humor and spirit, David Roche illuminates the potential in all of us to love and be loved by those around us. His voice, shaped by lessons that grace and faith have taught, echoes the importance of constant compassion for self and others."

—*Matthew S. Joffe, Vice President, Moebius Syndrome Foundation*

"David does not choose to write about the joy of overcoming difference but about the joy that is possible while living as different. He writes with such integrity that it seems unlikely that even 20 percent of him is insincere."

—*Gretchen Case, University Writing Program, Duke University*

"David Roche is revealing, intrepid and 100 percent funny."

—*Simi Linton, author of the memoir* My Body Politic

continued...

"David Roche captures a story so personal, so unique it hits at the very heart of what it means to be human. Wit, wisdom and whimsy blend with eloquent writing and evocative thinking that will be remembered for years to come."

—Victoria Maxwell, author, mental health educator,
Bi-Polar Princess (Crazy for Life Co.)

"Offer it up for the greater honor and glory of God—I never quite understood how suffering glorified God. Instead, I offer David Roche, not as sacrificial lamb but as testament to wit, to warmth, to wisdom. David is either the most spiritual comedian or the funniest sage I've ever come across. Or maybe he's both. Either way, I'll see you in church— the Church of 80% Sincerity. And I mean it."

—Jim Ferris, award-winning poet, Disability Studies Scholar,
University of Wisconsin–Madison

"In *The Church of 80% Sincerity*, David Roche weaves his moments of grace into the big picture and shows us that being different allows a person to make a difference." *—Christine Karlsson, Forward Face*

"*The Church of 80% Sincerity* is like hearing David Roche speak to you directly. He weaves his story with comedy and compassion in the way that only David Roche can do."

—Deborah Lewis, Executive Director, Ethel Louise Armstrong Foundation

"A talented performance artist, David Roche has written a lovely, lively, funny memoir of life with a facial deformity that has lessons for all of us about unconditional love, bravery, prayer and self-acceptance."

—Kathryn Montgomery, Director, Medical Humanities and Bioethics
Program, Northwestern University Feinberg School of Medicine

"This is an honest account of David's life journey that reminds us that we are all connected and all part of the same family. With his candidness and sincerity, David's soothing voice comes alive and the true importance of learning to love ourselves and seeing ourselves from the inside out is revealed." *—Allison S. Beck, enthusiast and friend*

THE
CHURCH
OF
80%
SINCERITY

David Roche

A Perigee Book

A PERIGEE BOOK
Published by the Penguin Group
Penguin Group (USA) Inc.
375 Hudson Street, New York, New York 10014, USA
Penguin Group (Canada), 90 Eglinton Avenue East, Suite 700, Toronto, Ontario M4P 2Y3, Canada
(a division of Pearson Penguin Canada Inc.)
Penguin Books Ltd., 80 Strand, London WC2R 0RL, England
Penguin Group Ireland, 25 St. Stephen's Green, Dublin 2, Ireland (a division of Penguin Books Ltd.)
Penguin Group (Australia), 250 Camberwell Road, Camberwell, Victoria 3124, Australia
(a division of Pearson Australia Group Pty. Ltd.)
Penguin Books India Pvt. Ltd., 11 Community Centre, Panchsheel Park, New Delhi—110 017, India
Penguin Group (NZ), 67 Apollo Drive, Rosedale, North Shore 0632, New Zealand
(a division of Pearson New Zealand Ltd.)
Penguin Books (South Africa) (Pty.) Ltd., 24 Sturdee Avenue, Rosebank, Johannesburg 2196,
South Africa

Penguin Books Ltd., Registered Offices: 80 Strand, London WC2R 0RL, England

While the author has made every effort to provide accurate telephone numbers and Internet addresses at the time of publication, neither the publisher nor the author assumes any responsibility for errors, or for changes that occur after publication. Further, the publisher does not have any control over and does not assume any responsibility for author or third-party websites or their content. The names and identifying characteristics of some individuals depicted in the book have been changed to protect their privacy.

First edition: February 2008

Library of Congress Cataloging-in-Publication Data

Roche, David.
    The church of 80% sincerity / David Roche.— 1st ed.
        p. cm.
    ISBN-13: 978-0-399-53390-7
    1. Self-actualization (Psychology)   2. Face—Abnormalities—Psychological aspects.   3. Roche, David—Religion.   4. Spiritual biography.   I. Title: Church of eighty percent sincerity.   II. Title.
    BF637.S4R63 2008
    155.9'16092—dc22   2007037227

PRINTED IN THE UNITED STATES OF AMERICA

10   9   8   7   6   5   4   3   2   1

Most Perigee books are available at special quantity discounts for bulk purchases for sales promotions, premiums, fund-raising, or educational use. Special books, or book excerpts, can also be created to fit specific needs. For details, write: Special Markets, Penguin Group (USA) Inc., 375 Hudson Street, New York, New York 10014.

Contents

Foreword *by Anne Lamott*   ix

INTRODUCTION   1

1. MIRACLES NOT ACCEPTED HERE   13

2. RANDOM ACTS OF CRUELTY   31

3. THE PRINCIPLE OF DELAYED UNDERSTANDING   45

4. THE BASIC MOTIVATING FACTOR   59

5. LIFE AS THE MIRROR   71

6. PRAYER   81

7. THE LAYING ON OF HANDS   95

8. UNCONDITIONAL LOVE HAS ITS CONDITIONS   113

9. PITILESS   127

10. FAITH AT RANDOM   139

Acknowledgments   145

Dedicated to Marlena.
With love, all things are possible.

Foreword

By Anne Lamott

I have loved this guy for a long time, and I think with the publication of this beautiful, marvelous book you will too. He may be like someone you've met before in your life, someone who has dealt with such serious illness or loss that he or she has been forced to do the kind of restoration that some of us suspect we are here on earth to do; who then takes you along into deeper understanding, the self-love that is so rare in this world, a person who can live equally in perplexity, love, resentment, peace and wonder. But if you haven't met someone like that, let me introduce you to David.

David and I met years ago through a mutual friend. The first time we spoke was on the phone and we talked about God for half an hour. He mentioned that he had some facial deformity, and I thought, well, whatever—maybe a little port wine stain, or an under-slung jaw. Then he came to my church, and it turns out he has one of the most severe facial deformities I've ever seen.

He was born with a huge benign tumor on the bottom

left quadrant of his face, which surgeons tried to remove when he was very young. In the process, they removed his lower lip, and then gave him such extensive radiation that the lower part of his face stopped growing, and he was covered with plum-colored burns.

He is in his early sixties now, with silvery hair and bright blue eyes. He came to my church a few times, and we talked a number of times on the phone about God and self-healing, our favorite topics, and he was funny. But it was not until I first saw him perform years ago, at a local community center at a benefit for the refugees in Kosovo, that I understood the extent of his artistic gift, which with this book you are about to receive.

He was wearing a dress shirt in plum purple, which exemplifies the kind of tender and jaunty bravery with which I have come to associate him—no neutrals for him, no senseless attempt to blend in. He was just right there, in deep self-respect, open to being seen and known, which is pretty rare even among people who look much more mainstream. He stepped out onstage before a hundred grown-ups and a dozen children, and stood smiling while people got a good look. Then he suggested we ask him, in a conversational tone and in unison, "David, what happened to your *face*?" I have so often wanted to ask people who have been through obvious physical trials how they came to look that way, and what it was like for them in there, and here finally was someone willing—no, thrilled—to answer.

Telling his stories through a crazy mouth, a jumble of teeth, only one lip and a too-large tongue, David's voice did not sound garbled but strangely like a brogue; like that of a Scottish person who just had a shot of Novocain. He spoke of the hidden scary scarred parts inside us all, the soul disfigurement, the fear deep inside that we're unacceptable; and while he spoke, his hands moved fluidly in expressions that his face can't make. His hands are beautiful, fair, light as air, light as a ballet dancer's.

From his experiences, he has built a church inside of himself. This book is an introduction to that church, an owner's manual for believers in soul beauty and the truth of our spiritual identities, a memoir by one gentle hero. There is no physical church but his own life: both his performances and his work teaching people to tell their stories, their marvelous, screwedup and often hilarious resurrection stories. Voilà: a church.

The stuff he talks about is such subversive material, so contrary to everything society leads us to believe—that if you look good, you'll be happy and have it all together, and then you'll be successful and nothing will go wrong and you won't have to die, and the rot can't get in. When David insists you are fine exactly the way you are, you find yourself almost believing him. When he talks about unconditional love, he gives you a new lease on life, because the way he explains it you may, for the first time, believe that even you could taste of this.

He has been married to a beautiful woman named Marlena for many years, and after listening to his lovely words, his magic, this doesn't seem at all strange. There he is, standing in front of a crowd, and everyone can see that just about the worst thing physically that could happen to a person has happened to him. Yet he's enjoying himself immensely, talking about ten seconds of grace he felt here, ten seconds he felt there, how it filled him and how he makes those moments last a little longer. Everyone watching gets happy because he's secretly giving instruction on how this could happen for them too, this militant self-acceptance. He lost the great big outward thing, the good-looking packaging, and still the real parts endured. They shine through like crazy, the brilliant mind and humor, the depth of generosity, the intense blue eyes, those beautiful ballet hands.

Welcome into the one True Church. It's the only church I've ever been to where they *want* you to wear your insecurity and messes and craziness and untrammeled confusion and screwed-up-ness on your sleeve; where they *insist* on your need to acknowledge your own magic and beauty. As I said, I think you are going to love this guy, and if you are anything like my friends and me, you are going to laugh, cry and want to join this church. One guess is that you will find some light for any path you happen to be on; one warning—that it will change you; and one recommendation, that you buckle up.

INTRODUCTION

I AM FACIALLY DISFIGURED. WOVEN THROUGH the left side of my face, head and neck, extending into my soft palate and airway, is a benign congenital tumor consisting of my own engorged and tangled veins and capillaries. My left cheek is tuberous and misshapen. My dark bluish purple tongue is twice normal size. When I was an infant, my condition was diagnosed as an extensive cavernous hemangioma. Sixty years later, as medical knowledge and diagnostic techniques have improved, it is more accurately described as a venous malformation.

My face is marked by surgeries. In early 1945, when I was fifteen months old, my lower lip was removed because it looked like a bunch of small Concord grapes and would not stop growing. I also was treated with heavy radiation as an infant; the idea being to retard the growth of the tumor. Those were the days when radiation seemed a possible miracle cure. Children with tonsillitis often had their tonsils irradiated. In my hometown in Indiana, the Highland Department Store had a machine in the shoe department where customers could x-ray their own feet. My friends and I often stopped in to play with this fascinating toy.

The radiation caused the lower part of my face to stop growing, giving my chin and jaw an unfinished look and leaving me with only a few teeth. Small gold capsules containing radioactive radon gas were implanted in my head. They were originally set in neat rows, but over the years they have migrated to different locations and are now a source of puzzlement and fascination to any health care provider looking at my cranial X-rays for the first time.

Throughout both childhood and puberty, I understood that I was never to talk about my face. I knew this because my disfigurement was never a topic of family conversation and, therefore, never considered a possible factor in my life experience. This denial served me well in many ways, because I was encouraged to consider myself normal. The price I paid was that I could never express any feelings about being disfigured.

It took me until well into my adult years to begin finding

my voice. Remarkably, I never talked about my appearance or my feelings about my disfigurement until I went onstage in my midforties.

I now make my living as a performer and public speaker. I have presented my signature one-man show throughout most all of the United States, including the Clinton White House, and I have performed in Australia, Canada, England, New Zealand and Russia.

I now talk about my face. I express my feelings about being disfigured. I share my voice. In this book, I do all three. But while this book has many stories drawn from my life, it is not my life story. It is the story of the Church of 80% Sincerity. It is the story of accepting yourself, in spite of all your flaws.

People ask me if the Church of 80% Sincerity is a real church. It's very real to me. It was clear to me that I needed an institution with rules to tell me how to behave and dogma to tell me what to believe.

I spent a good chunk of my life trying to live up to impossible ideals, starting with being raised as a Roman Catholic in the 1950s. My sense of guilt and failure was so strong that I concluded it would be impossible for me to live up to Catholic ideals well enough to get into heaven. Given that the most fleeting thoughts and merest desires could quickly qualify one for condemnation, I realized that, realistically, I should plan on going to hell. And make the best of it. We were taught in church and school to accept whatever suffering came our way—anything from itchiness to cancer to the death of a pet—and offer it up for the poor souls in purgatory. This would help shorten their waiting period to get into heaven. But I accepted suffering instead as a means to steel myself so that an eternity covered in flaming boils might be a little more tolerable. I thought this was prudent planning, though it certainly made for a somewhat dour worldview.

After a Catholic childhood, which included four years in a seminary, I spent ten years of my adult life trying to live up to the ideal of a dedicated Marxist-Leninist cadre. I barely noticed the transition. This time the paradise was to be an earthly one, but having an infallible leader was nothing new to me. Self-criticism was remarkably similar to confession and examination of conscience. There was plenty of self-sacrifice, with ideals impossible to achieve, and an approach to life filled with grim linear struggle and little joy.

By the time my Marxist illusions faded, I realized I no longer trusted idealists. To them, the ideal is more important than the human being. I began to look at life in just the opposite way, and that was the dawning of the Church of 80% Sincerity.

Soon after, I began to talk about my face. When I began to perform, I became part of a community of performers with disabilities. Slowly I stopped pretending to be normal and began to accept myself the way I was.

With that kind of background, who would not be drawn to an organization called the Church of 80% Sincerity? So I made it up—the church of choice for recovering perfectionists.

In the Church of 80% Sincerity, we think 80 percent sincerity is as good as it gets. (Especially in an election year.) You can be 80 percent sincere 100 percent of the time, or 100 percent sincere 80 percent of the time. It's in that 20 percent area where you get some slack and you can be yourself.

We also believe in 80 percent celibacy. Eighty percent compassion. And did you know the exact balance between healing and resentment should be 80 percent healing, 20 percent resentment?

It is the first postmodern church. We have no ideals. We do not try to change people by having them conform to an ideal. We try to accept people as they are. We adjust our beliefs and practices to conform to the reality of being human.

Take the practice of affirmations, for example. You know what affirmations are. "Every day in every way, I am getting better and better." Sure you are. You lie to yourself and lie to yourself until you believe your own lies. The only way that's different from denial is just that it's a lot more work. When I was trying to learn self-esteem, I was supposed to stand in front of a mirror, look myself in the eye and repeat, "David, I love you. David, I love you. David, I, I . . . Aargh."

I turned away because I realized I did not love myself. Luckily, by then I was a member of the Church of 80% Sincerity. We do things differently, more realistically. We don't try to change to measure up to an ideal. Instead, we adjust the affirmation to fit ourselves. I can stand in front of the mirror, and I don't even have to make eye contact. And I can say what I really think.

"David, you are a nice guy. You have a good sense of humor. I'm sorry, I just don't love you. I guess I'm not ready to make a commitment at this time. Maybe we could just be friends?"

In the Church of 80% Sincerity, I've learned to be friends with myself and to grow into and through my perceived flaws.

PEOPLE TEND TO FIND ME INSPIRING. THIS USED TO AMAZE me, in part because those of us with visible disabilities are often seen as inspiring, for reasons that have little to do with the reality of our lives.

It is not comfortable being inspiring. It entails too much responsibility. Thank goodness I had the prescience to call my one-man show *The Church of 80% Sincerity*, instead of *The Church of 100% Sincerity*. It gives me a natural out.

While I may inspire others, I am not too inspiring to myself. I look over my life and see that it is full of mistakes, misdeeds (intentional and otherwise), compromises, cowardice, substance abuse, failure to love, failure to risk and risks foolishly taken. The worst of it, in my mind, is that my misdeeds tended not to be flamboyantly risky but instead small, shameful compromises and evasions. I find myself wishing my sins had been sins of the heart and not sins of fear.

The truth is that I myself have always needed inspiration. When I was young, I admired Nellie Fox, the second baseman for the Chicago White Sox. "Little Nell" was short but he tried hard and did the best he could with what he had. I also looked up to the Mayo brothers, the doctors who started the Mayo Clinic, where I got my medical care. I saw them as living lives of service. And there was always the whole panoply of saints with their ability to endure pain. They were models for me in my practicing for hell.

Inspiration, then, does not have much to do with ideals. It is a basic human need. So, as the beloved founder of the Church of 80% Sincerity, it is my duty to be both flawed and inspiring. Eighty percent inspiring. (Ignore the man behind the inspiration!)

I AM ALSO DISCOMFITED WHEN PEOPLE SEE ME AS A PERSON OF deep faith. I am too aware of the many mornings when fear, doubt and resentment, after sitting all night by my bedside just waiting for the moment of my waking, make their predictions about the day ahead. Perhaps my faith, like a consumptive ingénue, is more attractive because of its delicacy and fragility.

One mark of a true religion seems to be faith in something patently unbelievable. I certainly have had that faith experience. In the Church of 80% Sincerity, however, you will find that faith is inconstant. But there are oases of faith in a vast internal landscape of doubt. And they can be found. Eighty percent faith usually lacks focus, but like all faith, it is worth striving for, because when encountered, it will stir the soul.

As a practicing member (indeed, the beloved founder!) of the Church of 80% Sincerity, I have come to accept my gifts as well as my flaws. And to see that sometimes they are one and the same.

In this book, I give you the principles behind the Church of 80% Sincerity so you can learn to accept yourself with your body's perceived imperfections and all your inner ones as well. I give you the hugs of my nana, the terror of my first boy-girl party, the man who spit in my face and called me the ugliest thing he had ever seen, the man who in dying gave me a moment of grace, the doctors who touched my face with detachment, the soul mate who learned about my face through touch, all the people who had faith in me before I had faith in myself—who helped me to find that inner beauty.

My face is unique but my experiences are wholly human. My face is a gift because I have been forced to find my inner beauty. That is a universal human need.

In this book, I offer you the gifts of courage, faith, inspiration and laughter that have helped me to accept myself the way I am, to understand that you and I are very much alike, with our gifts and our flaws as woven together—and as surprisingly beautiful—as the veins on my disfigured face.

ONE

MIRACLES NOT ACCEPTED HERE

I PREFER GRACE TO MIRACLES.

Whenever I have prayed for miracles, or expected miracles, or asked for miracles, I developed a frame of mind, or I should say a "frame of soul," that expected a dump truck to back up and tip a load of Lotto winnings on me. This hasn't happened yet. No miracle. Hoping for miracles always makes me lazy. And anxious. And just a tad resentful. And somewhat envious of people I consider unfairly rich or confident or content with life.

I do not believe in the instantaneous-totally-life-transforming experience. I do not believe in being born again. Or maybe I should say I believe that being born again is a lifelong choice that requires a good deal of effort. And grace.

We wish for miracles but the truth is that we have to choose and choose and choose again, and the karmic redemptive changes come slowly and in ways that we do not always understand. The good things happen a little bit at a time; we do not always recognize them as good. As we grow, as we accept ourselves as flawed creatures, grace is there to help us.

Easy for me to say now. But it was not always as evident. There were no miraculous bursts of understanding for me. There were, instead, long periods of narcissistic magical thinking and a constant blundering forward. And sideways and backward.

It was a long process of learning to recognize grace.

As a child, I could reel off a huge list of miracles, starting with Moses being found in the bulrushes, his staff turning into a snake, the burning bush, the parting of the Red Sea, manna and so on. Then came Jesus, with water into wine, the raising of the dead, blind can see, Lazarus.

I was given holy cards at school for being a good student. I studied the pictures of the saints on the cards. Saint Lucy was portrayed holding her eyeballs on a tray. She had plucked out her eyes because the emperor Diocletian had admired them and she was afraid that her eyeballs would be "an occasion of sin." She looked rather ecstatic for someone who was carrying around her eyeballs after gouging them out.

Saint Lawrence was pictured lashed to a huge grill. A Roman emperor was cooking him, again, this time Valerian. No miracle happened to save him. However, Saint Lawrence remarked during the cooking process that he was done on the one side and should be turned over. A miracle, then, could be found in having a good attitude.

Saint Sebastian is shown bound to a tree, his androgynous, hairless body dressed very scantily in a loincloth. A dozen arrows are imbedded in him. Sebastian's head lolls back, his face conflating suffering with orgasm. How's that for a good, miraculous attitude?

I could not make out what Saint Agnes was carrying on the tray in her picture. My parents were forced to explain that the tray held her breasts, which had been cut off by a Roman prefect because she had refused his sexual advances and would not renounce Jesus. No big problem for Agnes; she looked altogether calm and accepting.

There were also patron saints that performed miracles. Saint Anthony helped find lost things. If you buried a statue of Saint Joseph upside down in your backyard, you would get help selling your house.

I was surprised to discover a statue and a painting of Saint Roch in the Cloisters in New York not long ago. Turns out my namesake is the patron saint of the diseased, particularly those with plague. He is portrayed covered with open sores while a dog licks the ones on his leg. It seemed a little creepy until I read that the dog was actually an angel who cured Saint Roch of the plague by licking his sores.

What did I learn regarding miracles? It helped if you were one of the pathetically crippled, lame, deaf and dumb, horribly diseased or dead. They got all the miracle goodies. But it seemed that as soon as they were up and about, they would be susceptible to having their breasts cut off or be expected to gouge out their own eyes, with a cheerful attitude and an openness to the erotic possibilities inherent in the experience.

Those who were whole or normal were expected to yuk it up or dissociate while the rest of us suffered.

As a kid, I wanted a miracle. I felt that, with my disfigurement, I should be on the A-list with the diseased folks. But apparently that was not true.

I wondered, was it too much to make me normal? Okay, I knew that to change my face would be up there with throwing away the crutches at Lourdes, the holy shrine in France where the Blessed Virgin appeared. Or like Daniel in the lions' den. I thought I should give God a reasonable chance to show his stuff. To let him develop his skills. To warm up a bit. So, I occasionally asked God to help the Chicago White Sox win a baseball game or two. Especially against the hated Yankees.

God consistently failed to deliver anything at all miraculous. Not even an attempt, despite being given opportunity after opportunity. Many times one run, even one successful swing of the bat, would have been sufficient to convince me of the reality of miracles. Apparently, neither normality nor home runs were possible in my life. Most hideous of all, it seemed God wore a Yankee uniform.

I KNELT IN THE CHURCH. WITH THE STAINED-GLASS WIN-dows, that whiff of incense in the air, the echoes of the old Gregorian chant.

> *Pueri hebraeorum, portantes ramos olivarum,*
> *et clamabant dicentes: Hosanna, filio David.*

I prayed with my hands slightly open toward Jesus up on the big crucifix over the main altar. I prayed as sincerely as I could for beams of light to shoot out of the wounds of Jesus' hands into mine, so that I would have the stigmata, the wounds of Christ. I wanted proof that I looked the way I did because I was chosen and special. I wasn't even asking to look normal. But no, not even the tiniest laceration. No miracle.

As THE YEARS PASSED, MY MIRACLE LIST EVOLVED. BEGINNING in adolescence and continuing through early adulthood, the first item on my request list was the miracle of someone falling in love with me.

In 1966, I worked for Field Enterprises Education Corporation in the Merchandise Mart, right on the river in downtown Chicago. They published the World Book Encyclopedia.

I worked in the back room with Arturs and Danny. We worked an average of almost sixty-five hours a week. At night we were the only ones in the huge office and spent hour after hour trying to fill the ceiling light fixture with the rubber bands we shot at and into it. And we talked about women. Danny was a ladies' man. He had lots of advice for me, mainly that I should let my hair grow long like he did. Arturs was a Latvian immigrant. He had trouble with English but enjoyed practicing his skills with stupid double entendres that he explained with each use: "I feel good today. I think I could jump for joy. Jump for Joy. Get it?" I got it, especially after hearing it at least once a week. At Christmas, he leered when he commented that he liked the holiday because he enjoyed "feeling Mary."

I was desperate for female companionship. I considered myself much more sophisticated than Arturs, though I still operated at the emotional and social level of a thirteen-year-old at best. And I was imbued with all the sexual wisdom that the Catholic Church had to offer.

Debbie and her pal JoAnne were the two supervisors out on the floor. They sat together at coffee break and lunch, and I started sitting at their table. I liked Debbie. She was short, which I appreciated, and had kind of a cute body. Somehow, I became associated with Debbie. Not her boyfriend, not at all. We never dated. But in everyone's eyes—hers, JoAnne's, Arturs's—we were somehow connected. The only one who didn't know this? Me.

One day, blond, cute Pam was moved from the floor to a cubicle not far from where I worked. She started calling to me when I walked by her cubicle. I stuck my head in the door and she smiled winningly. She invited me to come in and sit down for a few minutes while she worked. She loved hearing about my work and my opinions.

Pam charmed me. I sat with her at break and lunch. I could tell that she also found me charming. We made dates to get together for coffee outside of work. Each time I arrived a few minutes early and waited and waited, making excuses for her in my mind. She never showed up. The next day she would explain that her hair had not been right, or that her mother wanted to talk to her, or some other ridiculous explanation, and I accepted whatever excuse she offered because she continued to be so charming.

Pam never did show up. That was when I started noticing that Debbie and JoAnne were snubbing me in the lunchroom.

Instead of an open chair at their table, there were turned backs. There were no miraculous love stories here.

But there was something different: grace. Ornery grace. It was present at Field Enterprises, even if I didn't realize it at the time. Making mistakes is how most everybody learns about relationships and the full range of human behavior. I was learning. No miracles, but grace—grace in my mistakes.

You can look for the grace years after making the mistake. It is still fresh, growing from the ground nearby, waiting for you to notice.

I MARRIED THE FIRST WOMAN I HAD SEX WITH. IT WAS MY Catholic training—I should have been going out on group dates at the pizza parlor. Joan had several good reasons why she wanted to marry me. For example, I had a good job as a computer programmer at International Harvester and had a sense of humor. My reasons were not as clear; however, I did believe that she loved me.

There was a tornado in nearby Oak Lawn on our wedding day, April 21, 1967. But I considered it a good sign that I had seen Pierre Pilote, the Chicago Black Hawks hockey player, in the bank on the day before the wedding.

Mostly, what we had in common was sex. Until she got pregnant a month after we got married. Our daughter Amy was born on February 22, 1968. Then we had parenthood in common instead of sex.

Joan soon tired of being the wife of an up-and-coming computer programmer in Forest Park, Illinois, so I applied to the graduate school of philosophy at Indiana University and got a fellowship. When we arrived in Bloomington, the philosophy department had been purged of "the Catholics" and taken over by logical positivists. Since I was not able to speak mathematics, I dropped out. It turned out the first semester's fellowship money would be better spent on mind-altering substances.

Joan and I were both drawn toward the counterculture. With Amy, we moved into a commune—a large house on Washington Street with a group of people who were into facial hair and drugs.

I thought I could be a hippie. I started letting my hair grow. Unfortunately, radiation therapy had left me with little to work with in the way of a beard. There was a patch on my chin that I thought had promise of becoming a goatee. But as the coarse black whiskers grew out, they swerved to the side to form a sort of hairy scimitar. I always looked like I was standing in a hurricane.

In the meantime, the Women's Liberation movement was moving toward more of a sexual liberation. It was smashing monogamy. And our marriage, which was fragile to begin with, turned out to be quite smashable. Joan and I separated in the summer of 1971. She moved on to San Francisco.

I stayed with three-year-old Amy in Bloomington, where it was becoming clear to me that I was getting attention that I was not used to from women. It seemed I was considered a model male. As the eldest of seven siblings, I had developed enough childcare skills to become a hit at the cooperative childcare center. At our communal home, I cooked and served the kids green scrambled eggs and ham and individual meat loaves molded in the shapes of their initials.

I too wanted to smash monogamy, or at least see what that was like, but I was very naive. I asked my friend Mark how a guy knew if and when a woman wanted to have sex. He told me, "Man, it is so simple. When their eyes get warm and kind of out of focus."

I was excited because I realized Mark was right. I had seen that look but I had not known what it meant. Now I knew that it could be more than mere friendliness. The only problem was getting up the courage to act.

NANCY VOLUNTEERED AT OUR COOPERATIVE CHILDCARE CEN-
ter. She had a cat named Rosa Luxembourg, so I knew she was politically sophisticated. I thought she was too beautiful to go out with someone who looked like me. I used up a year's quota of male courage in asking her out.

We went to a play, and then walked back through the southern Indiana summer night to the commune to sit on the front porch on our quintessential hippie couch with itchy upholstery. Bodily fluids and junk food effluvia had congealed into smooth patches where the upholstery had worn off. The couch's camouflaged steel prongs gouged the nether regions of sitters in retaliation for all the years of abuse it had endured at a dozen different student houses.

Nancy and I sat there and talked and talked about the play, about Amy, about the childcare center, all things that we had in common, all things that we were interested in. The conversation was going well, but I was growing catatonic with repressed lust. My left arm stayed rigid across the back of the couch for over two hours, pressing into that itchy upholstery, until one a.m., when Nancy said, "David, I think I need to walk home now."

The moment froze. I fell back into feelings and fears from when I was twelve. What really was happening was that, of course I wanted to kiss her. But I thought, here I am, a monster with only one lip, what right do I have, who would want to kiss someone who had a lip surgically removed? I didn't even know if I could do it right. I fought the panic and something bubbled out of me: "But I want to kiss you."

Nancy turned to me and said, "Oh, David, I thought you were never going to ask."

And there it was: a moment of grace. Even after being

married, it was the first time in my life I realized that I was attractive to women, that I could be sexy.

It turned out I could kiss well. On that old couch, we melted into one another for hours. I absorbed the smell of Nancy, musky, with acrid armpit reek, a rosemary shampoo halo and the patchouli that pervaded everything and everyone at that time. Around us wafted the smell of dew on the grass, the aroma of pizza from Romano's over on Walnut Street.

After some time, I became vaguely aware of people walking by on the sidewalk, about fifteen feet away. I stopped. I opened my eyes. I looked at Nancy. She had evidently ceased being an active partner some time ago. Her hands were behind her head. She was regarding me with a slight, amused smile. The moment of grace had been extended into the night.

IN LIFE, YOU NEED TO BE ALERT JUST IN CASE SOMETHING good does happen. Those times when you realize that life is good only last about half of a second. They are not as sweeping or dramatic as miracles. They can slip up on you quietly. They can be ornery. They can be disguised. They can be very scary. In your whole life you only get a total of maybe four minutes of these moments of grace. You have to learn to grab on to and extend the moment.

As you journey through life, sometimes God opens a door and says, "David! Look! Nancy likes you." The door is open. If you hesitate, if you say "Huh?" *Bam!* The door slams shut. Too late. You missed your moment of grace.

When that door opens, push your foot in. Tell God exactly what you want. "I want to kiss her. Now, please."

The great thing about grace is that it happens whether you have a good attitude or not. You don't have to even believe in it. But it does help to recognize it.

IN 1987, DURING A TIME OF DEEP SPIRITUAL CRISIS, I COULD only express my feelings with obsessive physical activity. In the gym, I whanged away at the Nautilus machines, wanting only to hear the metal clash and clang. At home in the Day Street house in San Francisco, I labored in the garden out back.

I was pretty much a Catholic gardener, fiercely devoted to the identification and eradication of evil weeds. My house-mate Gary took care of planting and nurturing while I pried out the oxalis from in between patio bricks and dug to get at the deepest roots of the blackberries.

A neighbor had given us some Sweet 100 cherry tomato plants—the only kind of tomato that will grow in foggy San Francisco—and they needed to get into the ground. I put them near the brick wall against which they could be supported and where they would get the most sun. After watering the new arrivals, I got on my knees and began weeding the area. The sun was out as I labored. As I rested for a moment, the sun seeped through my shirt, my skin, my flesh and into my bones. I looked at the tomatoes. I knew they would not miraculously become the kind that grew giant and juicy and furrowed by rain, like in Indiana where I had grown up. But I did have the faith that they would grow, and that I would grow with them. I tried to get up, but for a few moments, I couldn't. With the sun's warmth penetrating me, the seeds of faith and hope growing inside me, there I was, caught and held by grace.

AROUND THIS TIME, MY DREAMS STARTED TO CHANGE. FOR most of my life, my standard recurring dream was the anxiety dream. The scene changed; sometimes I was a student, sometimes at work. Always I had failed in a responsibility and was about to be held accountable, and I would wake craven and shivering.

Until this dream came:

I am looking out a large window. The sun is shining. Its very bright light is coming into the scene at an angle. It highlights many small insects and dust specks floating and darting about in the air. There are many single-strand spiderwebs being caught and blown sideways by a breeze. There are some wisps of what seems to be smoke. The breeze is coming from the left.

I am enchanted and delighted. I realize that what I am seeing is not insects, webs or smoke, but grace. I have been granted a vision of grace and can see it permeating, suffusing, streaking through the world about me.

A woman comes in a door. She is dark-skinned, with black hair. I approach her and remark on what I have seen. She smiles and acknowledges me and my vision. She talks. Though I do not understand her language, I know she is telling me that she has known about the grace for a long time, and that it all comes from Mary.

I tell her, "Yes, yes. Like Ave Maria." She agrees. I want to find words to describe to her what I have seen, but they are not quite there. I want to get out the words, *gratia plena* (full of grace). I think she may understand the Latin, but the words do not emerge. I am filled with wonder that stays with me as I awaken.

The miracles I believe in are minimiracles, manageable miracles, bite-size miracles, miracles lite, one-minute miracles. They are miracles built of dreams, built of tomatoes, built of kisses, built of choice after choice in the face of uncertainty and fear. They are miracles built of grace. As we open to grace, we are miracle makers.

TWO

RANDOM
ACTS
OF
CRUELTY

People often assume that I had a miserable childhood, that I was constantly taunted, fearful, isolated and shy. For some reason, it is difficult for them to believe that I was reasonably happy as a child.

Let me say it clearly: I had a happy childhood. Puberty was a different story, but my childhood was good.

My parents, informed by their Catholic faith and, just as deeply, by their own fundamental decency, were supportive and loving. I was encouraged in most ways to strive to be my best.

My mother always told me: "David, you are so smart! You could be anything you want to be." She said it so often that I believed her. Part of this was simple post–World War II upward mobility. But at another level, I entered each day feeling that I was a whole person, a child of God.

I was almost always in a safe place: in the neighborhood, in school, in church, with my family. I felt valued and normal. Once in a while I noticed another mother asking my mom about my face and she would reply with something about "a birthmark."

I was never brought into these discussions. I was uncomfortable standing off to the side, but I listened carefully so I could learn how to explain myself. But I never learned to explain myself. Instead, I learned the safety of standing to the side, the safety found in not saying anything.

THERE WAS NOTHING DAINTY IN OUR HOUSE WHEN I WAS growing up: no carved wood, no crystal or porcelain on display, let alone in use. Everyday items had to be able to take significant abuse, and that included our Christmas crèche.

It had been purchased, like so many of our household accessories, from the Ben Franklin in downtown Highland, Indiana. Made entirely of plastic, Jesus, Mary, Joseph, the two angels, the donkey, the oxen, the lambs and the three Wise Men (two white, one black) all toppled to the floor frequently during our games and squabbles. Whenever that happened, we accused the offender of having committed a mortal sin before semireverently reconstructing the scene.

Our Baby Jesus came already safely molded into his plastic manger. All you could see of him was his face and hair; the rest was covered with crisscrossed plastic swaddling. His hair, of course, was bright yellow. His eyes were large and blue, lips pink. He looked like a decorated Baskin-Robbins ice-cream cone. The eyes had been stamped on by a machine somewhere in Japan and were askew, the left one slightly higher than the right and gazing about ten degrees in a different direction. His pink little mouth had also been imprinted just a little west of where it should have been.

In our house, since nobody talked about the fact that my face was disfigured, I never revealed that I secretly loved this Baby Jesus, whose face, I thought, looked a little bit like mine.

WHEN I WAS ABOUT NINE, DAVID JOHN PORTER CALLED ME "jughead." That confused me. I thought I did not look at all like Jughead from the *Archie* comics.

"It's because your head is crooked, your face is crooked. You're a jughead."

"It's not crooked. I don't look like a jug."

At the time, I did not experience this as cruel, only foolish. No one else picked up the nickname.

* * *

THE FAMILY STORY GOES THAT, WHEN I WAS NEWBORN, MY great-aunt Rose leaned over my cradle and said, "This boy is destined to be a bishop." Of course every great-aunt Rose of every firstborn son in every Irish Catholic family throughout the country leaned over the cradle and said the same thing.

At Our Lady of Grace School, boys were constantly encouraged to listen for God's call to be a priest. The girls listened for the call to a nun's vocation. We learned in school that what priests say is the word of God. The nuns told us, "Children, if you saw an angel and a priest walking toward you on the sidewalk, you should greet the priest first, because he is God's representative."

I was smart. I was an altar boy. I was a good boy. So at age thirteen, after all this buildup, I decided I wanted to study to become a Catholic priest. This was in the days when thirteen-year-olds were commonly accepted to seminaries.

On a May day in 1957, my father drove me to South Bend, Indiana, for an interview with the Holy Cross priests who ran the seminary at the University of Notre Dame. As an Irish Catholic boy growing up in the Midwest, any affiliation with Notre Dame and football was desirable. We sat in an office with two priests. They seemed very kind and very grave. I told them that I loved Jesus. I told them I thought I had a vocation to be a priest.

They left the room. My father and I looked out on the green Notre Dame campus. He pointed out the golden dome.

The priests returned a few minutes later and said, "David, we do not think that you have the call to be a priest. Because of your appearance, people would not respect you as a priest."

I looked at my dad. I could see he was angry. I twisted my hands. I held back my tears. I had been nervous about being accepted to the seminary, but never expected to hear the voice of God telling me I was a monster. All that had come before—the love of my parents, the belief that I was valued—crumbled inside me. I stood frozen and ashamed.

On the way home, my father was angry. He pounded the steering wheel and muttered, "Those bastards." Later, we didn't talk about it.

AFTER BEING REJECTED BY NOTRE DAME, WE FOUND ST. Lawrence Seminary in Wisconsin, "The Poor Boy's Seminary." I knew that I would have a place of refuge, a safe place for my shame to hide. I stayed there for four years but never escaped that feeling of being a monster.

I did not talk with anyone. Inside myself, in my adolescent fantasy life, I secretly worked on a speech wherein I would announce that I was marked because I was the illegitimate son of Adolf Hitler, the world's most evil man who was punished by God for his sins by having a disfigured son.

After four years, I left St. Lawrence. It was not a good hiding place for me.

WITH ADOLESCENCE, I BEGAN TO CHANGE. ON THE BUS, IN restaurants, in all public places, I started to move to the far left rear of the room so that my bad side would not be as readily seen.

I avoided new stores, any places where I could encounter strangers unless absolutely necessary. Only the safe environs for me.

The older I got, however, the more difficult it became to find safe places.

IN MY EARLY TWENTIES, LIVING IN CHICAGO, I DECIDED FOR some reason that I wanted to go to a singles bar. Of course I was terrified. Who wouldn't be, disfigured or otherwise? But the terror was buried down deep and could always be diminished with alcohol, which became my accommodation to my unspoken-of disability.

It was a balmy evening in Chicago. It had rained during the day and as I walked along the sidewalk in Old Town, waves of moist heat rose from the pavement. As I tried to walk into the bar, a huge bouncer blocked my way. He was drunk; his breath had enough alcohol to sterilize an operating room. He grabbed my arm, burst out with laughter, pushed me back against the wall and held me there, on display. He turned to the crowded bar and yelled, "Hey! Hey, take a look at this! Look what is trying to get in here!"

A hundred pairs of eyes turned to stare at me. Behind the bouncer stood Andy Flaherty, an acquaintance from college. I nodded to him, "Andy." The bouncer doubled over with laughter. "He's a friend of Flaherty's! A friend of Flaherty's!" Andy turned away. The bouncer let go of me. I stumbled to the bar, ordered a double tequila on the rocks, downed it and left.

LATER IN MY TWENTIES, IN THE LAST MONTHS OF MY MARriage to Joan, I helped to found the Childcare Switchboard and Single Parent Resource Center of San Francisco. We were the pioneer childcare informational and referral agency in the country. I worked there for eight years as a phone counselor. Part of my job was site visits to childcare programs. On a visit to the Mission Childcare Consortium one day, the teacher was busy. I went down the hall to wait in an empty classroom. As I examined the exhibits of macaroni stuck to construction paper with Elmer's Glue, something hit the back of my left knee from behind. My knee buckled, sending me into involuntary genuflection. I turned to face half a dozen boys aged four or five years old. They were coming at me in karate poses and started to yell, "Monster,

monster! *El Monstro!* Kill him, kill him." I ran away as fast as I could. I told no one what had happened.

When I was about forty, still living in San Francisco, something different happened.

I was walking down Market Street on my way to my job. Out of the corner of my eye, I sensed a figure coming in my direction. The movement was strange because the figure was headed toward the up escalator that I had just stepped off. I registered the strangeness. A man—I knew this because of the shoes and pants in my field of vision—moved in front of me. I hesitated in order to let him pass. But he did not move. I looked up.

A handsome, young black man, slim and coffee-colored, stood in front of me. He was well-dressed, and looked to be maybe a lawyer or a salesman from the men's department at Macy's. I stopped, startled, just beginning to take in the situation. Because of the way he was dressed, because of his looks, I was not alarmed. I met his eyes. They were gray green. He took a quick step toward me. His face contorted and he spit in my face. He said loudly, angrily, "You are the ugliest thing I have ever seen." He stepped around me and walked on down Market Street.

I fumbled in my pocket for a Kleenex. I wiped my face. The crowd kept moving around me.

And then, this is what happened: I yelled at his retreating back. Without planning, without thinking, I yelled, "You are ugly in your heart."

He was far enough away that he probably did not hear me. But in that moment, with my spontaneous response, my face still damp from his spit, I stopped standing to the side.

AT WORK THAT DAY, I TRIED TO FORGET WHAT HAD HAP-pened. Tried to close it off, put it immediately into the past, focus on the present. By this time, though, it was harder to summon up a sense of denial. Partially because of the cruelty, the degradation and humiliation of being spat upon, certainly.

But more than the shock of the assault of saliva and mucus and the verbal abuse, my response surprised me. What was radically different, what was more startling to me than his random act of cruelty was the fact that I had reacted almost instantaneously this time. It signified a sense of self-esteem and power that had been dormant since childhood.

I mulled it over all day.

Art, a good friend from seminary days who was visiting from Milwaukee, was waiting for me when I got home that evening. I told him what happened.

Street confrontations were neither new nor particularly shocking to Art. What he had to tell me was based on decades of experience working with inner-city, homeless, impoverished people in Milwaukee, many of whom had been diagnosed as mentally ill. And Art worked with them with love and commitment.

"Dave, if you could look inside that man, you would find a great deal of pain. I am not saying, not in any way, that such a stupid and cruel thing was right. Can you see that he acted entirely out of a sense of his own worthlessness and ugliness?"

"Art, the thing is, he was not ugly at all. He was handsome."

"Makes no difference what he looked like—you came close to the mark with what you said to him. If he were coming to me as a client, I would be looking for that feeling of ugliness inside him."

The thing that struck me, even more than what he said, was that he spoke calmly, reacting to the spitter's actions as if they were well within the range of normal human behavior. I paid close attention. I began to reframe that experience of cruelty. When I spoke to my tormentor, I claimed my own being, my inner worth. What Art told me opened another door.

A COUPLE OF MONTHS LATER, I WAS ON THE SAME UP ESCALAtor and my handsome fan was about thirty feet away on the down escalator. He spotted me, pointed and shouted, "Hey, look, it's Freddy Krueger! Hey, Freddy Krueger!" I felt myself scanning for inner shame and finding none. This time he had little effect on me. And he was too far away to spit at me. I was going up. He was going down.

I HAVE BEEN CALLED JUGHEAD AND EL MONSTRO. I HAVE been told that I was too ugly to be a priest and that I was the ugliest thing that a man had ever seen. For a long, long time I stood off to the side, hiding myself, unable to voice my feelings. I stood to the side and heard these things.

Now I can say that the plastic Jesus looked like me, that I thought the priests were representing a cruel and judgmental God.

Now I do not stand off in the shadow. I can speak. And I can hear more clearly the subtext of cruelty, the same inner voice of unworthiness that speaks in me.

No, I do not condone cruelty, and I know that it exists in many, many worse forms than insults on the street. But I do understand it better, in the sense that it is in all of us. And once I began to understand, I was no longer so entangled in the web of my own fears.

I know now that my face does not belong to me; it belongs in a catalog of symbols. The face is often (falsely) seen as the locus of the human persona. When it is scarred, it becomes a reminder that the entire human experience is one of being flawed. It is not the fact of my disfigurement that wears at my psyche. It is the fear and self-doubt of others, their very human concern about their own social acceptability, their worry about being unloveable and abandoned, which they project onto me through their words, through random acts of cruelty.

I do believe that we each have a place inside of us where fear resides, that fear of being unworthy, a sinner, carrying bad karma, untouchable. Seeing and accepting one's "flawed" condition is a core spiritual experience, an essential step in developing emotional maturity. It is a basic human task, the task of redemption, and it is hard work. There is no turning aside. If we ignore this soul retrieval work, we remain fragmented and powerless, vulnerable to fear, addiction and the metaphor of victimhood. Because that place of fear is where predators and manipulators of all sorts—sexual, financial, religious, political, warmongering—come to feed. And that is where cruelty is born—in fear of not being acceptable, worthy, valued and loved.

Paradoxically, I have found wholeness through (and with) what at first seemed to be my flaws. Working through my fear and shame, I have come to discover that I am whole.

I know now that when people turn away, they're not turning away from my face, but from themselves, from their own fears.

When they meet me in the light of day, all their fears are pushed onto me in a millisecond. And that's my job, to carry the weight of that fear for them, to carry it so we can all pretend we are normal, if just for a bit.

THREE

The Principle of Delayed Understanding

As a child, Halloween always brought me joy: it marked the official beginning of sugar bingeing season. A full month ahead, I stashed two of the highest quality shopping bags from Marshall Field's under my bed. They were sturdy, with strong handles, and easy to open so there would be no time wasted with clumsy fumbling. Days ahead, I noted the official starting hour of sunset, and planned my route to maximize the take of candy.

In seventh grade, I was invited to a Halloween party at Mary McDermott's house. I was very excited. I was only invited because Mary's mother, Betty, was my mother's best friend, but I didn't know that then. I knew I'd have to limit my trick-or-treating because of the party, but I wasn't too concerned—I was anticipating bowls full of candy corn, circus peanuts and little Oh Henry! and Baby Ruth candy bars.

I decided to dress as a clown. I had a great outfit, a hand-me-down from a neighbor—homemade, one-size-fits-all baggy, with big polka dots made of iron-on Bondex. I found a seventy-nine-cent clown-makeup kit at the Ben Franklin store. My father's basketball shoes completed the outfit. I knew I looked good. I had my Halloween groove going. That is, until I walked in the door at Mary's house.

In six or seven heartbeats, my whole world changed.

I first noticed Bob Gallo. He was supposed to be a pirate. Bob's costume consisted of a yardstick in his belt and an eye-patch that he wore above his eye rather than over it. I looked around the room. Everyone else had costumes that were vastly more adult and sophisticated than mine. Mary Lou Francini looked like she was ready for the prom. Only the tiara in her hair made it seem at all like a costume. The Keilman twins had cowboy hats but no cap guns. Clearly no one else had been trick-or-treating.

Then the full realization came like a hammer to the heart. Unbeknownst to me, I had arrived at my first boy-girl party—in full clown drag.

This was far beyond feeling that my face was different. This was landing on a different planet without a space suit.

You probably can guess the first game that we played. You're right: spin the bottle.

And you probably can guess the first spinner. Remember Christine from seventh grade? The cutest girl in the school? Blond, blue eyes, pink fuzzy sweater. She had no costume, only a Lone Ranger–type mask. Most important, she had recognizable breasts. Not breasts that were too big, like Alice Murphy's, or too fat, like Agnes Touhy's, or too tiny, like Mary McDermott's, or falsies, like Angela Matovich's. Christine's breasts were just the way they should be.

We knelt in a circle in the McDermotts' basement. I stared down at the brown tile floor. Christine spun the Coke bottle; it rattled round and round. Its movement was mesmerizing. It began slowing down. Slower, slower, seeming to taunt people as it went by them. Then, oh my god, yes, it pointed right at me.

I looked across at Christine, who looked me straight in the eye. My spirit shrank. Her lip curled. She said: "Oh. Yuck. Not you." She reached down and spun again.

I knelt there with a roaring in my ears. I looked right back at her and said, with complete confidence, "Christine, I know you want me."

The whole circle went "Oooooh." Christine looked shocked, then slightly chagrined. Barbara Gordon giggled. Everyone waited for Christine's reaction. She colored slightly, then looked at me shyly. I stood up and reached out my hand.

She took it and we headed off to the closet for our kiss as all the kids cheered.

ACTUALLY, THAT LAST PART IS A LIE. I DID INDEED SAY, "Christine, I know you want me." But I said it twenty-five years later. What really happened on that Halloween night was: I knelt silent and still while Christine spun the bottle to find someone else.

It only took me twenty-five years to find the right words to say to her. When I said them, Christine was not there. Neither was anyone else. But I still said it. That delay is a perfect example of the Principle of Delayed Understanding.

THE PRINCIPLE OF DELAYED UNDERSTANDING, A GUIDING principle of the Church of 80% Sincerity, states that you cannot understand what is going on while it is going on. We are big fans of this in the Church of 80% Sincerity. Contrary to New Age belief, consciousness always lags behind reality. Here is proof: How many of you are still trying to figure out things that happened in your childhood, twenty, forty years ago? The best you can hope for is to minimize the length of time it takes to catch on. Perhaps this is not clear to you? Well, there you go. More evidence of the truth of the principle of delayed understanding.

When you think you understand what is going on while it is going on, you are most likely delusional.

This is simply a statement of reality and frees us up from the need to pretend, to beat ourselves up for not knowing the right words or actions. Don't worry about not knowing the answer immediately. Don't confuse yourself with Google. For that matter, remember that Google does not know the right answer either; it just spits out information quickly.

The principle is a way of acknowledging that it takes time to let down our past barriers to understanding, and to the entry of grace.

EARLY ON A FOGGY AUGUST MORNING IN 1974, I SAT IN THE waiting room of the Hemangioma Clinic at UCSF. The generic waiting room was windowless, with dark orange Naugahyde furniture.

I was there to put myself—or to be more precise, my face—on display for students in exchange for medical care. I dreaded this periodic visit and always took a Valium on the mornings of my appointments.

That morning, I was the only adult patient in that waiting room. Most of the rest were infants and small children from all over northern California. The nursery-school-age children were too young to have much of a sense of their own facial difference, any awareness of the bright red violet outbursts on their faces. But the unfamiliar surroundings and their parents' tension signaled that something was askew. They sucked their thumbs and grabbed their mothers' skirts or fathers' pants for reassurance. Only occasionally would they head to the play area of the waiting room.

A young man wearing a white coat appeared at the door carrying a small camera. He read from the chart in his hand: "David . . . Roche?" My eyes still cast down, I followed him along the corridor that reeked of floor wax. His shoes squeaked. On my right, windows with a view of the green band of Golden Gate Park, the Golden Gate Bridge, the Pacific surf churning strips of foam against the Marin Headlands. To my left, the corridor walls, with portraits of important men, former department heads and chiefs of dermatology. I felt as if each of them was diagnosing me as I passed by.

The man with the camera led me into an empty examination room. I knew what to do. I unbuttoned my shirt and pulled it open. I turned away briefly to remove my dentures, wrapped them in tissue and stuck them in my pants pocket. I turned back to the camera and posed, offering a variety of angles and shots. I knew he wanted to see everything. Mouth shut. Mouth open. Tongue out. Tongue lifted. Tongue to the left, tongue to the right.

There was no conversation, no sound except the camera's click, the flash's pop and crinkle. The pervasive smell of burned-out flashbulbs overpowered that of alcohol and adhesive tape. There was no eye contact. He looked at me only through the lens. When he lowered the camera, I knew he was done. I replaced my teeth and my shirt and returned to the waiting room.

After another interlude, I was ushered into a large, echoey amphitheater. About thirty men and women sat in rows above me. I was able to classify them according to facial expression and posture. Physicians and dentists leaned back, objectively assessing. Social workers nodded to convey their understanding and warmth. Surgeons had the least affect. With their narrowed eyes, they searched incessantly for incision sites. A couple of the younger ones flushed slightly when I looked at them; they had not yet learned to mask their faces well.

Doctor Torrey was in charge. She introduced me by reciting a summary of my medical history.

One by one, they came forward to examine me. Some grasped my tongue with a piece of folded gauze, pulled it out, and gently turned it to expose all sides to view. I stared straight forward at blue patches with the UCSF logo, attached to pockets that held penlights and drooping stethoscopes. My breathing grew deeper. My examiners stepped back a few paces and talked to one another in soft tones that let me know that I was not supposed to hear, let alone to respond. If our eyes ever met, it was only a nanosecond before theirs turned away with easy, practiced avoidance.

As they probed, I closed my eyes and slid toward a hibernative state, the place where I had learned to go in these situations. My sense of self retreated to my core, where it waited, pulsing and watching. The hands that touched me were soft and gentle, smelling slightly of Betadyne. These hands were the only ones that ever touched my face. Even with the clinical detachment implicit in their touch, I secretly savored the physical contact as it rippled through my body. I moved slightly, in concert with their touch, leaning toward it. Shame-charged parts of me were being caressed.

After about ten minutes of this peculiar intimacy, the physicians returned to their seats. Doctor Torrey addressed me directly: "Well, Mr. Roche, it seems that you have made an excellent adjustment—"

At that moment, a short bark erupted from my throat. Torrey stopped in midsentence. Her eyes widened. Heat suffused my chest. One, two, three seconds passed.

I channeled rage that I did not know was there. I choked out, "Don't talk about adjustment! You don't know! You don't know! Touch . . . my tongue. You never . . . You never talk about feelings . . . or anything!" I stopped. My ears roared. The doctors stared, locked into a combination of shock and scientific observation. My throat throbbed. I rocked slightly on the stool. My mouth was dry. I wanted to urinate.

All the others turned to Doctor Torrey. She was the only

one looking directly at me. "Perhaps you would like a referral to a psychiatrist, Mr. Roche?" I gulped, shook my head. She said, "Thank you." The examination was over.

I stood. My legs were weak. I walked out of the amphitheater, through the waiting room to the elevator and then out into the San Francisco fog. My mouth tasted of metal.

Although I didn't realize it right then, at age thirty, for the first time in my life, I had begun in those inchoate moments to talk about what it felt like to be facially disfigured.

WE DO NOT UNDERSTAND WHAT IS GOING ON WHILE IT IS going on. The human soul does not wear a watch, has no way to keep track of linear time and no interest in doing so. It waits patiently for us to gather the grace and the tools to understand childhood embarrassment, human frailty, the qualities that we mistakenly feel are locked forever in our past.

And to be clear, it is not just pain that can be locked away. The times when joy or pride cannot be expressed in the present, they are recorded in soul time too, still available in their fullness when we are ready to accept them as part of who we are.

We are not failures for not understanding what is going on when it is going on. We simply do not always have the tools.

In the Church of 80% Sincerity, we believe in self-kindness. It takes years (by conscious reckoning) to learn the hard stuff, to learn what it is we need to learn, to know that the moment will come when it will, and while we are waiting for it, we should be kind to ourselves, and to others too, for they are in the same state.

It does not mean that time has passed, only that the moment has expanded.

Who says a moment has to be so tiny anyway? Who exactly are the moment police? In the Church of 80% Sincerity, you are allowed to say how long your moment is. So in June I can obsess about something I did in January and still be living in the moment. Or maybe your whole life is just one moment and all you have to do is live in your life to live in the moment.

So you see, it did take me just a moment to find the right response to Christine.

I AM ONCE AGAIN IN THE AMPHITHEATER AT THE UNIVERSITY of California. The walls are still green. The lighting is the same. Yet it feels much warmer. The audience looks very different to me this time around. They are not a blur of white coats. There are certainly more females and a few more minorities than there were a quarter century ago. Even the elder physicians look different. Their faces are more relaxed, their eyes warmer and less penetrating. I wonder if there are any present who were there twenty-five years ago.

I am sure that I, too, look different and more at ease.

This time there is no waiting room, no photographs taken. I am the only patient. Introduced as an expert on the physician-patient relationship, I deliver a lecture entitled "Facial Disfigurement: The Patient's Perspective." I use my own story from all those years ago as an example of how physician-patient communication can begin. This time, the questions are directed to me. Afterward, I receive a standing ovation. The doctors come up to me again, not to poke and prod, but to express appreciation.

I DID SAY, "I KNOW YOU WANT ME." NOT TO CHRISTINE, BUT I said it.

A quarter of a century had passed, but my soul still hung waiting in that moment of the spin-the-bottle game, waiting, just waiting for the right response from me. My soul did not care about the passage of years, never looked at a calendar or a watch. In soul time, it was still the same moment. The moment had expanded until I could fit into it, until I could find my voice.

I found it in the amphitheater as a guest speaker, years after my first visits as a patient. I found it when I met my future wife, Marlena, when I knew she wanted me and I wanted her. I continue to find it onstage, in the pages of this book. The moment is now.

FOUR

THE
BASIC
MOTIVATING
FACTOR

In the Church of 80% Sincerity, we understand that the basic motivating factor for all human beings is not self-preservation or sex or love. It is the desire to not be embarrassed. Psychologists tell us that the number one fear of all Americans is the fear of public speaking. The fear of death is number six. (Which is probably why capital punishment does not work too well.)

Behind the fear of embarrassment is that deeper fear, of saying what you really think and feel and telling your story, because that is when you may be exposed as stupid, inarticulate, selfish or anything else that you would rather leave undiscovered.

*   *   *

IN 1978, I WAS A COMMUNIST. WE WERE NOT DEDICATED TO overthrowing the government. (I think you may have us confused with Rush Limbaugh.) But we did want to change the world. I was doing political organizing with San Francisco's Grass Roots Alliance. We were campaigning against California Proposition 13 and wanted to get out the vote. I decided I wanted to help the cause of changing the world (for the better) by standing up and giving speeches on the city buses of San Francisco.

My denial combined with my commitment to a cause did not allow me to acknowledge that my appearance could be an issue.

I decided I'd speak on my regular morning bus—the number 14 Mission—when it was filled with a captive audience of working-class San Franciscans of all sorts, just the voters we wanted to reach. Latina *abuelas.* Janitors. Women who worked cleaning on arthritic knees. Mothers with babies in slings. Seniors dressed in winter clothes from the 1950s, still thinking that they were wearing their good coats. Men who reeked of paint. Lots of 49ers and Raiders sweatshirts. Giants caps. I planned to be the last one on the bus, so that after I paid my fare, most of the other passengers would already be seated. Then I could grab on to a pole, steady myself and speak from the front of the bus.

Each day, as I waited to get on, my legs grew numb with fear. I knew I was going to make a fool of myself, that I would be mocked, punched, arrested, scorned. The little man in the back of my brain tried to encourage me in his own inimitable way: "Come on, Roche! You can do it. What, are you a goddamned chicken? Wimp! Petit bourgeois coward!" There I was, a disfigured man, stumbling along in the inner city, pale and sweaty, clenching my hands and cursing under my breath, forcing myself forward.

For two weeks, every day, I climbed up the bus steps, hesitated, cursed my cowardice again, and crept to the rear of the bus. Eventually, I think that the numbness in my legs moved up to my brain, erased the fear and allowed me to act, because one morning I got up there, steadied myself and began, "Good morning. My name is—" I stopped.

All those faces were looking at me with stunned expressions. Fear pushed the words back down my throat. The passengers were too surprised to be annoyed. I was familiar with the look on their faces, that of absorbing and assessing my face.

A well-dressed gentleman was sitting near the front of the bus. He was white, and looked polite, middle class, interested. I dimly remembered something about looking one person in the eyes while speaking, so with a lurch of courage, I kept eye contact with him and started up again. As I did, the man stood, swung his briefcase at me and screamed: "Get off the bus, you deformed faggot!"

He missed me. I turned and looked at the driver, a heavy-set black man with his maroon and khaki Muni uniform and cap. He looked straight ahead.

I don't remember for sure, but I believe I babbled on for a while. My fan taunted me. I don't know how long I talked or what I said. When I stopped, I only knew that I had failed. I couldn't look at anyone. I made my way to the back of the bus, humiliated. My inner little man spoke up sarcastically: "Congratulations, Roche!"

I sat there, miserable. But then, a hand appeared in front of my face. A woman's hand, puffy and pale, with a few liver spots. For a second I believed that it was my Aunt Rose come to comfort me. I stared until I understood that this hand wanted my hand. I looked up at a gray-haired woman in a light green coat. She clasped my hand and patted it encouragingly. Her cheeks shook a bit as she spoke in an Irish accent, "You did a grand job, son. A grand job." She turned, took a step toward the front of the bus and yelled at the heckler. "You get off the bus. Get off, you damn bully."

I was stunned. Another hand grabbed my left shoulder, coming from the seat behind me. A larger and darker hand. I turned. Two Latino guys, "vatos," in what I took to be their gang outfits: Pendleton shirts buttoned to the top and hair-nets. One of them stood up, reached over and grabbed my hand. He said, "Yo, homey. All right. You did a good job, man. A good job. But you know what?" I quavered, "What?" and he continued, "Hey, look, you see some more people been get-ting on the bus." He reached behind me, grabbed my belt, lifted me a bit up off the seat and gave a firm shove out and into the aisle. "Man, you got to get up there and do it again."

I looked to the front of the bus. The heckler from hell was leaving. I did do it again. When I finished, applause rippled through the number 14 Mission as it pulled away from the Thirtieth Street stop.

I CAN'T SAY MY FEAR WAS NOT WELL FOUNDED, BECAUSE I DID indeed feel horribly, miserably embarrassed. If I could have foreseen that heckler's reaction, I never would have gotten up there. Never.

But my embarrassment was only in me, not in the others who saw and heard me. They gave me credit for the courage it took to stand up there. I spoke about a dozen more times, each time getting a positive reaction from the other passen-gers, especially from those in the back of the bus. No driver ever tried to stop me.

THREE MONTHS LATER, I SAT IN THE FRONT PEW, FEELING nervous. My colleague Candace was next to me. Not only was I the only white person in the Third Street Baptist Church, I was probably the only white person for half a mile around.

This was not familiar Sunday morning territory for me. This was not like being at Mass. Not at all. Here, people were talking in church. A lot. And singing. A lot. Catholics sang tentatively, if they sang at all. Here, the whole congregation was involved in the hymn, the choir moving and shaking, the band carrying a heavy beat. The whole place thrummed.

We sat down again and I grabbed my script. I would have three minutes at the pulpit to talk about getting out the vote to defeat Proposition 13 and I wanted to do it right. The Grass Roots Alliance had a special invitation from Reverend Kennard and we wanted to cement our relationship, in addition to bringing out voters. I kept running through the script in my mind. Each time I forgot something and got more nervous.

Reverend Kennard began to introduce me. It was not a simple introduction. After a few sentences, his voice started to rise; his cadence became a powerful one. I realized he was charging the crowd up, getting them ready for me. I kept repeating the words of the first sentences of my talk over and over in my head.

The Reverend gestured to me. "Please, please welcome our guest into the house of the Lord."

I stood and walked up the two steps onto the riser. As I did, I felt the heat of the church, the energy of the full congregation at my back, pushing me up and forward.

Reverend Kennard reached out two hands to take mine and welcome me. He was formally turning over his pulpit. As I moved to the pulpit, I suddenly became very aware that I was exposing my left side, my bad disfigured side, to everyone in the church.

At that moment, I remembered a black girl about thirteen or so, standing with her friends outside James Lick School on Clipper Street many years before. I had walked by the group and heard her say loudly from about five feet away: "Eew. He gross."

Eew. He gross. Eew. He gross. Eew. He gross. Over the years, I had turned that into a chant, a mantra of embarrassment that had a life of its own, that appeared in the middle of the night, a refrain that echoed and reinforced my diminished sense of self, of how I appeared to others but never ever talked about. On the way to the pulpit I heard it in my head again and began to feel sick to my stomach. Eew. He gross. It drew me like a siren song, the lure of succumbing to its familiarity instead of the vulnerability of exposing myself to embarrassment.

At the pulpit, I looked out at a full church crowd of close to two hundred. I could not fully focus; it was like looking at a moving abstract painting. People—mostly women—were shouting. I saw waving hands, elderly folks, some standing, all well dressed, some swaying.

As I kept looking out, individuals in the crowd began to stand out and the scene no longer felt abstract. I was waiting for silence but instead kept hearing:

"Yes, Lord."

"Praaaiiise the Lord. Praise Him."

"Thank you, Jesus."

Those waving hands were all preparing the air, preparing each other, casting a glorious spell, encouraging me.

And my feeling of ugliness, of being a freak, of being gross—they all washed away, and I was being baptized, baptized in a sea of love and support. I did not choose to take it in. Instead, it picked me up and shook me; it bypassed my brain with its list of words and went right to my heart.

I spoke and gave the energy back. I had no recollection of what I was supposed to say, none at all. They brought it out of me. Whenever I paused I was renewed by "Amen. AMEN." And "That's RIGHT! Tell it. Tell it, brother." They called forth grace and banished embarrassment.

I stood there in that loving energy and knew I was in the presence of God, right where I was supposed to be. I knew that I could never, ever turn back again.

AND THERE WAS GOD. NOT GOD UP IN THE SKY, NO BEARDED old alcoholic bipolar man with a rigid smile on his face and a club behind his back. Only community, the feeling of mutual support and being in it together and the first great glimpse of what my life could be.

It was God from below, a lower power, a power lifting me up, not pushing me down, supporting not suppressing, encouraging not intimidating, cradling me, wanting me to be my best, not counting my sins born of fear and dread.

MY FEARS ABOUT SPEAKING WERE CONSIDERABLE. I THOUGHT that my difference separated me from others, that my face was an impediment, that it would be a reason for people to scorn me.

Amazingly, that fear turned out not only to be unfounded, but also to be the opposite of the truth.

What I feared is not unique to me alone, but totally human. We all fear that we will be embarrassed, that we are not acceptable to others, that we will be rejected.

The story that you have to tell, the message you have to convey, may not seem unusual to you. But the things I have to say are not that unusual either. It's the same old thing: love yourself, find your sources of faith and work them, nurture relationships, keep trying.

We each have the responsibility to help each other tell these stories, to remind those in our purview of the things that we all already know—that people are basically good as well as flawed, that the barriers are in our own minds. We have to keep reminding and reminding and reminding each other to keep telling our stories, to remind ourselves and each other that the fear of embarrassment turns out to be a predecessor to grace.

FIVE

LIFE
AS THE
MIRROR

THE FIRST TIME I EVER GAVE A TALK ABOUT facial difference, a lovely woman came up to me afterward.

"David, I just had to come up and say what your talk meant to me. You . . . You are so courageous. And inspiring. You know, people tell me I am attractive. I think I have, well, normal looks. But when I was in junior high, it was terrible; I was so embarrassed about my freckles. And tonight, when you were talking, I remembered that, and I realized that I am still very ashamed of my freckles. When I am having a bad day I feel like just scraping them right off my face."

I was stunned. I had to turn away for a few seconds. I felt a surge of scorn and thought to myself, "Oh really? The heartbreak of freckles?" Then, in a burst of resentful anger I thought that I would love to slap those freckles off her face. But I did not say anything out loud to her.

When I first started speaking in public, people talked to me after my show and said, "David, you changed my life tonight." I was courteous, but a big part of my internal response was, "You are pathetic. One show changed your life? You should get a life."

I had no respect for them. I did not take them at their word. I wore the armor of arrogance. I had no respect for myself, for what I was doing. I did not believe that someone like me could ever be inspiring.

But then I delivered a keynote speech to an organization of adults with learning disabilities. They too were part of the generation of denial. I was not sure why they had invited me to speak. Wasn't their experience totally different from mine? They all looked like normal, successful people.

They were rapt as I spoke and when I finished, they rose in a spontaneous standing ovation, many of them crying. I listened, then, to their stories, which were about hiding their true selves, about being ashamed of not being able to read, about not having any idea that they had dyslexia, or even that there was such a thing as dyslexia. They had to work much harder, always trying to hide the fact that they could not read, dealing with accusations of laziness, carrying this burden their whole lives.

And I began to understand that I lead life as a mirror. People see themselves reflected in me.

AFTER A TALK, A GENTLEMAN APPROACHED ME. HE WAS stocky, middle-aged, wearing a University of Michigan sweatshirt. His hair was thinning, his face a little jowly. As he came closer, I could see that he was very moved; his eyes were puffy and red. He didn't say anything at first. It seemed that he was too choked up. He reached for my hand and held it with two hands, pumped it up and down, leaned in toward me and whispered, "I know what you are talking about. Believe me, I know." He stood straight up, nodded solemnly, squeezed my hand and turned and walked away, wiping his eyes.

MARLENA AND I GAVE OUR "LOVE AT SECOND SIGHT" TALK TO an elementary school. In the talk, Marlena told about what it was like for her when she first met me, how angering it was when people stared at me and whispered comments to one another behind their hands.

Most of the students streamed out of the amphitheater after we were done. A few stayed to say hello, to express appreciation.

A young girl about twelve years old came down out of the amphitheater seats. She was stiff with nervousness. She came up to Marlena, stood in front of her for a moment and then reached forward to embrace her. She put her head on Marlena's shoulder, shuddered and began to weep.

Her girlfriends crowded around her. They said to Marlena, "Her dad died and she is sad." The girl, unable to look up, still sobbing, nodded her head. Marlena held her for a long moment.

The girl's father had died during the summer. When she returned to school, the other students did not know how to talk about her father's death and neither did she. She found that they would point at her and make whispered comments to one another. Their intentions were not cruel, but still, the girl felt like a freak on display. She never talked at school about those feelings, or about her father's death, until Marlena's story opened her up.

The girl's friends started brushing and braiding her hair.

After Marlena and I finished another school session of "Love at Second Sight," I saw a young girl lingering off to the side. She was slightly chubby, a little young looking, but not unusually so. Her face had an earnest sweetness and intensity. She began to talk to us, looking to see if other children were listening.

"I had this thing, like a wart, but the doctor called it something else, like a virus, on my hand, right here, you can see where it was."

I really could not tell where it was, so just responded, "Hmm," and she went on.

"The doctor put white stuff on it. Anyway, at school, Myra, my friend—this was last year—saw it and said, 'What's that? Eew, it's gross.' Or whatever. Yeah, she said it was gross. I told her not to call it a wart. It's a virus. She said, 'Is it contagious?' and I said it was, and I was going to say, 'Not very contagious,' but she screamed, 'Lindsay has cooties. Eew. Get away, get away.'"

"Cooties," I said.

She rolled her eyes. "And all the girls ran away from me and wouldn't come near me until the wart—the virus—went away. One boy, Daryl, pretended to touch my hand and then die."

I HAD JUST FINISHED A PERFORMANCE OF *THE CHURCH OF 80% Sincerity* at a small theater and was sitting in the dressing room. The stage manager, a stunningly attractive woman, appeared at the door.

"Hey, great show. Good house. They loved it. Can I come in?"

"Thanks. Sure. Sit down."

As soon as she sat down, her face changed. She started to sob.

"Oh, I'm sorry, I'll leave. Oh, God. This is so discouraging."

I motioned to her. "Wait, sit, sit. It's okay. What?"

"I watched you work tonight, it was great, but . . . This is awful, I know . . . but, well, I have been considering disfiguring myself. Do you think that's crazy?"

"Well, it doesn't seem like a good idea to me. What is going on?"

"I want to be a director. Nobody takes me seriously because of my looks, my body. It drives me crazy."

She began sobbing again.

"I just want to cut my face, a scar or something. I get so tired. If I did not look like I do, my life would change. I think you must know what this is like. You must, don't you?"

I HAVE LEARNED THAT THE FRECKLED LADY, THE WOMAN who wanted to cut her face, the man who had struggled through school to adulthood with an unnamed learning disability, the children suffering teasing for myriad minor physical differences, all of them saw aspects of themselves in me. I am no longer allowed to feel different. Instead, I realize that I am you, enhanced.

* * *

MY FACE IS AN ELABORATELY DISGUISED GIFT FROM GOD. OH, not a gift I was ecstatic about receiving. Did I open this gift and say, "Ah . . . ah! Exquisite! How did you know what I wanted, God?" No, it was more like, "You shouldn't have."

But my face is a gift, because my shadow side is on the outside where I have had to learn to deal with it. I know that other people are inspired by the simple fact that I have learned to deal with it, and that I accept myself. And as much as I have learned to see myself as I am, and to have faith in myself, I also see mirrored the beauty of others—especially those who share their stories with me—to accept them as flawed just as I accept my own flaws.

I look in the mirror nowadays. Certainly I do not let my tongue hang out as it sometimes does because it is swollen. Certainly I do not drool. Certainly I do not let the left side of my mouth droop down as if I had a stroke. Certainly I do not let my left eye be so much larger than my right eye.

But I make eye contact with myself. I lock in on my own eyes. I tilt my head slightly, I look again at myself, I smile a certain smile. Instead of hoping for a miracle, I am more able to see myself as I am (at least eighty percent of the time). I look myself in the eyes and practice being charming. My friend Margaret says that I charm myself. That sounds about right.

SIX

PRAYER

G ROWING UP, THIS IS WHAT PRAYER MEANT
to me:

1. Rote memorization. If a nun said to me:
   "Hail Mary, full of grace, the Lord is with
   thee. Blessed art thou among women and
   blessed is the fruit of thy womb, Jesus," I
   would automatically spill out: "Holy Mary,
   mother of God, pray for us sinners, now
   and at the hour of our death. Amen." Find a
   Catholic who grew up before Vatican II and
   whisper in her ear, *"Dominus vobiscum."*
   Her answer will be: *"Et cum spiritu tuo,"*
   after having heard this reiterated a thousand
   times at Mass.

2. An approved list of things I had to believe in to go to heaven. Good Catholic schoolchildren knew exactly what they believed in. There was a certain awesome power in hearing hundreds of children repeat in unison: "I believe in God, the Father almighty, creator of heaven and earth, in Jesus Christ, His only Son, our Lord, who was conceived by the Holy Ghost, born of the Virgin Mary, suffered under Pontius Pilate, was crucified, died, and was buried. . . ."

3. A formalized expression of regret and apology. The nuns at Our Lady of Grace School prepared the eight-year-olds for our first confession. My turn came. I entered, knelt at the screen and began: "Bless me father, for I have sinned. This is my first confession. I disobeyed my mother five hundred times." I thought I heard a grunt on the other side of the screen. Maybe five hundred was a little high, but I wanted to vacuum out my soul. Then I confessed that I had committed adultery nineteen times. The nuns and priests had not bothered to explain adultery to the eight-year-olds. Fortunately, my cousin Eileen had explained that adultery was a terrible sin in the eyes of God, and that when you farted in church, that was committing adultery. I saw a bare calf with a black sock on it rise up from the other side of the confessional screen as the priest roared with laughter. I jumped up and left, my adulteries unforgiven.

4. A political act. Every school morning at eight a.m., all the students at Our Lady of Grace appeared at Mass. After Mass, Father Alvin remained at the altar and announced prayers "for the conversion of Russia," thereby obeying the requests made by the Blessed Virgin in her appearance at Fatima, Portugal, in 1917: "If my requests are heeded, Russia will be converted and there will be peace; if not, she will spread her errors throughout the world, causing wars and persecutions of the Church. The good will be martyred, the Holy Father will have much to suffer, various nations will be annihilated."

5. A commodity. I was eleven years old and looking for a Christmas gift for my great-aunt Rose. The rack of Spiritual Bouquet cards caught my eye, and I picked one up. On its front, a standard sort of Catholic picture of a boy kneeling in prayer. Winged cherubs hovered nearby. The boy gazed up at a figure of Jesus up in the sky. Jesus had his garment open as well as his rib cage and sternum so you could see his heart and it had a cute little crown of thorns on it and a dagger stuck in it, and there were a few drops of blood coming out. The caption under the picture read "A Spiritual Bouquet Especially for You." And inside, you could list the number and the types of prayers that you were promising to say for that person: five hundred Hail Marys, two hundred and fifty Our Fathers, one

hundred rosaries. I realized that I could promise anything I wanted and no one would ever know if I had said those prayers. The thought was so disturbing, so powerful, and so sinful to me that I put the card back and stepped away. But, desperate for a present, I turned back and bought two of them. I wrestled with the dilemma for a couple of days but when I weighed all the factors, I decided that over the course of my life I probably could accumulate that many prayers for Aunt Rose. She was delighted with the gift.

6. A family happening. For quite a few years, in the 1950s, my family knelt in the living room and prayed the family rosary together. Adept rosary sayers could whip through a rosary in six to eight minutes, easily. There was a constant social pressure to speed up. The prayers went much faster with the elision of consonants, vowels, syllables, words and whole sentences: "HailMryflvgras (Hail Mary, full of grace), Thlordzwthee (The Lord is with thee), Blezdarthoumungwmn (Blessed art thou among women), Nblezdizthfrutvthywmbjez'z (And blessed is the fruit of thy womb, Jesus). . . ."

7. A punishment. In the seminary, there were always a few boys in the back of the chapel during morning Mass, waiting to go to confession. It was very clear that we were the masturbators. It was the same thing, time after time:

"I touched myself in an impure way." And the same denouement each time: "*Ego te absolvo.* Your sins are forgiven. Go in peace and sin no more. For your penance say ten Our Fathers and ten Hail Marys." Each time, I'd walk out of the confessional and quickly say my prayers, counting them on my fingers, amazed at the lightness of my penance compared to the possibility of an eternity in hell.

8. A disappointment. My great aunts who were nuns had sent us a bottle of blessed oil from the shrine of Saint Joseph in Montreal. When I was alone in the house, I would sneak into my parents' bedroom and get the oil out of the wardrobe where it was kept. I smeared a few drops on my face, praying that God would remove my hemangioma. He didn't.

9. A routine, like brushing my teeth, but much less useful and understandable.

By the time I was eighteen, I stopped praying.

WHEN I WAS MIDDLE-AGED, I HAD TO LEARN TO PRAY AGAIN.
    In the fall of 1988, my friend David was in the last months of his life, dying of AIDS. I flew from San Francisco to Los Angeles at least once a month to care for him.

I was afraid.

I was afraid of what I saw. His beautiful, warm brown eyes looked the same as always. David had been a large, burly, hairy man. Now AIDS had taken away his strength and his flesh, leaving jutting bones and the biggest diaper I had ever seen. He had given up trying to lick off the white stuff that congealed in the corners of his mouth.

I was afraid of what I smelled. The smell of shit was awful and pervasive in the room, but when I drew closer to David, the metallic reek of the meds on his breath was worse. It took a while to realize the unfamiliar dominant smell was the omnipresent smell of death, of necrotic cells and wasting tissue.

I was afraid of what I touched. My hands on David felt no flesh; they went from skin to bone.

I was afraid of what I heard. His voice came only on the raspy out breaths.

I was afraid of the taste on my lips when I kissed his forehead.

In my fear, I wanted to know the rules for how to behave, how to be a good friend. I wanted to help.

"Hi, David. What do you need? Just tell me. Anything. What should I do? I know. Jell-O. I'll make Jell-O. We'll have Jell-O. We have lime or black cherry. Which would you rather have?"

"Just be here."

"There's Cool Whip!"

"Just be here."

As weeks went by, this sort of interchange continued, me struggling to figure out and do the right thing, never quite sure what he was talking about. I thought he was not in touch with his needs, or perhaps was too shy to request the help he needed, or, most likely, he had something they called dementia that I had heard of but did not understand.

It took me a couple of months to catch on that he was totally in touch with his needs, and what he wanted was my full presence. Jell-O was not as important as just being there. I learned to shut up and we spent hours together saying nothing at all. Except when we watched Kirk Gibson hit his home run off Dennis Eckersley. David yelled and I groaned.

One Sunday night in January, after I had been there for a while, I packed my suitcase, ready to leave for work the next morning. David and I sat on the couch together, his head on my lap. The Mass in B Minor was on the stereo. I was stroking his forehead. His eyes were closed. Occasionally, pain broke through the drugs and made him twitch and gasp. Mostly he was silent and dozing. Then I felt his body slowly gathering energy. He smacked his lips, trying to bring moisture to his mouth. He opened his eyes and stared at the far wall for a very long moment, then turned his head toward me and asked if I would stay for the rest of the week.

I drew my hand away from him.

"Oh. Oh, I would love to but I can't, not on such short notice. I, if I called in, I couldn't, 'cause I'd just be fired. I couldn't just . . ."

I stopped.

I was flooded with a sudden knowledge.

Just be here.

The old rules slipped away.

I said, "Yes."

David took my hand back, kissed it, held it to his heart and said, "Good for you."

He closed his eyes and turned away, breathing deeply. He dozed off. I could feel his heart slowing in my hand.

That was the last week of David's life. It was the first week that "Just be here," and "Good for you," took root as prayers in my heart, the first to lodge there in many years.

IN 2001, WHEN I WAS ABOUT TO GO INTO THE HOSPITAL AND expected to be in the ICU for a week, I asked all my friends to send me love and support. In response, I was offered chanting, meditation, Masses, rosaries, positive thoughts, good wishes, dedications of performances, poems: in other words, prayers of all sorts.

At first, I did not recognize what I was given as prayers. Then, in the week before surgery, I was awakened night after night with dreams that reinforced one theme: I was loved.

The first dream: While I take a nap in a bus, a group of African American teenagers surprises me by painting the interior of the bus for me.

Two nights later: I am enjoying visiting a museum with a family in Mexico.

The next night: I am working in a sewing factory with Asian American women and I am pleased when my Chinese boss promotes me to sewing beautiful dresses.

And again: I am at the first rehearsal of a new play, working with talented actors who are delighted that I am part of the ensemble.

They were the sweetest dreams that any mother could wish for her child, each dream engendered by prayers that came to me through my unconscious. As the surgery grew near, a strangely exultant streak ran through me, a confidence born partly of not believing I would die and partly of the loving support that moved through me. And again, prayer proved itself to me without my asking.

Now prayer is real to me again, woven through my life in new and wonderful ways.

This is what prayer is to me now:

Prayer is not a planned thing. Prayer emerges of its own accord. You are not supposed to pray. You are supposed to get out of the way of the prayer that prays itself.

Prayer is not words—not spoken words, not written words. Prayer is about relationship. Prayer is the expression of relationship.

Prayers can be sobs and caresses.

Prayers come in the bathroom, in the shower.

Prayers come in the middle of the night, when you jerk awake and your first thought is of the worst time you made a fool of yourself; your second thought is of how you are failing at whatever you are doing in life; and the third thought is not a thought but unfocused resentment. And you say, "Fuck! What the fuck am I going to do? What the fuck? What the fuck? *What the fuck?*" And you say that a hundred times and it becomes your rosary.

Don't be ashamed of rough, vulgar prayer. God likes you that way. God likes you vulnerable. You are not editable in God's eyes.

Some prayers are prepared for God like a formally posed photograph. Yes, you look nice in that studio photo and that is the image you want God to see. But God does not look at the photo from the studio. God looks at the photo that, when your friend who took it shows it to you, you say, "Oh, my God, I look so weird. That is not me." And your friend says, "No, no, that's one of your 'looks.' That is so you!"

And you have to realize that your friend loves you that way, not the way that you have learned to present yourself for a photo, standing rigidly, with your head tilted charmingly just so and with the sly, cute smile. No, your friend loves you when your mouth hangs open because you are tired, when you have tea stains and spinach on your smile, when your dentures are yellowed. God is not fooled by teeth whitener or Botox.

To pray, put aside the fruit of the tree of the knowledge of good and evil. Pray from your reptilian brain, where words are misspelled and mispronounced and there is no punctuation and you are not polite and you weep and gnash your teeth.

What do you say to yourself? Here are some things I say when I am in the shower, as I prepare for the day ahead, as I slip into fearful, anxious mode:

"I want to go to the store. I want to go to the store."

"Please don't hurt me. Please don't hurt me."

"Please, God, help me do this right. Please, God, help me do this right."

I don't know why I say these things. I don't know where they come from. They have been coming up for years. Maybe they are essentially meaningless. I repeat them over and over and I find myself saying them many times, many days, with no reason that I know, without choosing to say them.

I believe that these are my basic prayers. They're what I have to say to God.

When I say, "I want to go to the store. I want to go to the store. Please don't hurt me. Please don't hurt me. Please,

God, help me do this right. Please, God, help me do this right," they are the primal prayers of the disfigured little boy who wants to show that he is normal. That his behavior is appropriate. That what he does is of value to others. That he has emerged from the shadows with gifts in his hands for all.

SEVEN

THE
LAYING
ON OF
HANDS

IN 1986, MY YEARS AS A TRUE BELIEVER IN
Marxism had come to a close with the col-
lapse of the Democratic Workers' Party from
within due mainly to corruption and rampant
alcoholism. I was in deep crisis. I weighed 115
pounds. I was drinking a lot of Royal Gate
lemon-flavored vodka. I smoked two packs of
cigarettes a day. Morning food was doughnuts
and coffee, lunch was burritos, dinner was the
vodka. I was emotionally and spiritually bereft.
I spent a lot of time pondering my life deci-
sions past and present, accounting for them,
searching for answers and direction.

In my yoga class, I met Karen, a massage
therapist with long black hair and a Botticelli

face. I told her, "Oh, I've been thinking of getting a massage." She said, "Come see me. Don't worry about money." She was offering me a free massage out of the goodness of her heart! I made an appointment on the spot.

I lay on a table that seemed like an examining table, but Karen's hands held no bright metal, no scalpels, no bandages, nothing that reeked of alcohol or any medication. There were no bright lights, no buzzing or clicking noises, nobody standing a few feet away talking about me. As she worked, forty years of my muscles being held at attention changed in a few moments. My judgments, my rules, my ways of looking at the world, they all fell away.

At the end of the massage Karen went to the foot of the table and held my feet with her thumbs pushing gently into the soles. A current, a low level electrical shock began running up my legs toward my heart. I asked her what she was doing and she said she was sending a prayer from her heart to my heart. That was how I began to believe in the healing power of touch as loving prayer.

I came to her for a massage every couple of weeks for almost two years. After the first two months, I quit drinking. After eight months I enrolled in massage school.

Touch is one of the corporal works of mercy, a material beatitude.

There are five ways that people give and receive love: spending quality time, offering service, giving compliments, giving gifts, and touching. We had touched a lot in my family of origin, but it was most often the low-level violence of contact sports. Nurturing touch was new to me.

The value of touch for me, especially at this time of my life, was that it held me in place, in the moment. When I was being touched on the massage table, I could not stay in a state of resentment and anger about the past actions of others. I was not able to feel guilty about my own past choices. Similarly, I could not look to the future with fear and anxiety. Anxieties that often ballooned into fears were touched out of existence.

WHEN I FIRST MET MY FUTURE WIFE, MARLENA, WE DID NOT get off to the best start. The first time she saw me, she was so surprised by my disfigurement that she turned and walked away without saying a word.

Things like that happened to me every once in a while. I was used to the sequence. A look of shock lasting anywhere from one to three seconds, followed by either an attempt to recompose the muscles of facial expression into the kind of blank look which today's Botox addicts strive for, or else a look away to something purportedly more interesting, such as a crack in the sidewalk or a scan of the sky for possible falling comets. In this case, I took it as a positive that Marlena's shocked expression had changed to one of outright honest embarrassment before she turned away.

For the fifteen years since my marriage to Joan had ended, I had been in relationships lasting from a few months to a couple of years, but nothing I considered permanent. By the time I was in my early forties, I had decided I was comfortable being single. Those secret feelings from adolescence, the belief that no one would ever love me and that I was incapable of love, had taken deep root. One reason was that, incredibly, I had never talked about my appearance with any partner, aside from my standard one minute summary: hemangioma at birth, surgery, radiation, doesn't hurt, it's all okay.

During that time, I did decide at one point that I had been too reactive to women, that I needed to determine what it was I might be open to in a relationship. As usual, I made my list—a very detailed one that worked along a wide continuum. For example, I wanted someone who would have respect for my faith and spirituality and its Judeo-Christian roots, not someone who was into the New Age spiritual Prozac. And I wanted someone cute.

As I proceeded to elaborate and construct the perfect woman in my imagination, I realized how very judgmental I was being. I wondered what right a disfigured man had to want an attractive woman. I had to think about that for a few days. Then it came to me: I did not necessarily need, or even want, someone with particular physical characteristics. I just did not want someone who felt bad about herself, someone who would be constantly obsessing about her physical flaws. In that regard, I wanted someone like me.

THE DAY THAT MARLENA AND I MET, WE WERE BOTH LEARN-ing to give massages to terminally ill and dying hospital patients at Pacific Presbyterian Medical Center in San Fran-cisco. Marlena claims that I did not remember her on that day. But I did. I really liked her gentle manner with the patients. As well as her freckles. And her cheekbones.

She and I also volunteered to be part of the task force founding the first massage therapy program in a hospital in the entire country. We worked together in an environment of healing, service, community and collaboration, seeing each other at our best. Though she was married, we became close friends, building a friendship with kindness and mutual regard.

I brought her my homemade winter fruit curry. She gave me a book on the Olympic Peninsula rain forest. When I met her mother, Lillian, for the first time, Lil said, "My, you and Marlena are kindred spirits, aren't you?"

Marlena observed my habit of eating a half pint of Häagen-Dazs every night and offered me nutrition counseling. Under her guidance, I switched to eating frozen yogurt, then low-fat frozen yogurt, then nonfat frozen yogurt.

Slowly, surely, sweetly, I was drawn to Marlena. I denied it for a long time. I certainly was not looking for a relationship with a married woman. Yet, every day, she held a larger place in my imagination. Yes, she was cute. Five-feet-two-inches tall, just over one hundred pounds, merry dark brown eyes, with the energy of a hummingbird and the grace of a born dancer. Marlena exuded soul. More than anyone I had ever met, she consistently looked for and found good in others. At times this seemed much too Pollyanna-ish, but it was always genuine and certainly was a great counterweight to my tendency to view life as class struggle. Besides, she was always willing to look at me positively too.

WHEN MY FACE IS TOTALLY RELAXED AND IN REPOSE, MY left eye stays slightly open. My left cheek bulges and sags. The left side of my mouth droops as if I had a stroke. My mouth hangs slack and open, showing my two lower front teeth. My purple tongue protrudes slightly. I usually attempt to arrange my face in an approximation of normality. Effort goes into closing the left eyelid just a little more, holding up the left side of my mouth, squeezing the muscles on the left side to keep it from sagging, holding my mouth closed, hiding my tongue and teeth. It is a constant, unremitting, minimally conscious effort that causes no end of stress and headache. It is the physical counterpart to my emotional denial, this ludicrous and essentially useless effort to appear symmetrical.

Marlena got to know my face by touch.

When we practiced what we were learning in the hospital, Marlena spent a long time on my face. Her gentle hands went to and held those tense armored areas and each time, slowly, slightly, a bit of armor was discarded. I would arise from the massage table looking my true normal self. I began to care less and less about putting the facial armor back on—at least with Marlena.

I SAW SOME OF MARLENA'S FLAWS TOO, THE THINGS THAT SHE tried to hide. When she and Larry moved across the Golden Gate Bridge to Mill Valley, Marlena wanted to build her massage therapy practice there. She showed me a letter she intended to send to friends and prospective clients. I was dismayed at the lack of self-confidence it showed. Marlena was a world-class body worker but her letter was almost apologetic in its tone. I stewed for a few days, trying to figure out how to respond. What I had to say about the letter was critical. What I had to say about her work was complimentary, encouraging and very personal. As I drafted my written comments, I realized I was revealing my love for her. I decided I had to give her my best, so I wrote an honest reply.

When she read it, she sat and cried in her car. That was my first conscious act of love for Marlena. It was the equivalent of her touching my face. She accepted and touched my outer disfigurement; I accepted and touched her inner disfigurement.

The routines of my life remained the same. I lived in a small apartment on the ground floor at Day Street. The bedroom window had a view of the garden framed by night-blooming jasmine. I went out there and comforted myself by obsessively pulling up weeds. Then I stopped working and just let it be. I was learning to catch and savor the moment. My being, my consciousness, was no longer in my head. My contact with the earth let it drain down into the rest of me, and the worries and stresses went away with it. I silently held my hands in the earth, marveling at how it was drier and warmer on the very top. I stayed there like a lizard in the sun. I stared dumbly down at my own hands in the earth. After a while I turned my head, like a lizard turns his, and I looked at the tomato plants brimming with red fruit.

After David's funeral, I came back to San Francisco with an envelope containing a lock of his hair and faded jacaranda blossoms from his grave. My world had been shaken by my time with him. I was looking at my soul, holding it up to the light, waiting to see what was different. As David had waited to die, all that mattered to him was love. His example unsettled and inspired me. I did not want to wait until the last months of my life to be open to love like that.

THE FIRST TIME I SAW MARLENA AFTER I RETURNED FROM David's funeral, we had scheduled an hour's massage for me. Marlena lost track of time and worked on me for two hours as I slipped in and out of a trance. When she started, I held my shoulder blades up around my ears. After I awoke from the first trance, my shoulder blades had relaxed but were trembling, unsure of what to do. When I awoke next time, my shoulder blades were flat against the table, in their natural resting position, where they stayed.

In those two hours, my life had changed. Marlena had brought my heart to the surface. As my body relaxed, I shuddered and wept. Her healing hands reached inside me and rolled away the rock that I had in front of my heart.

I knew that love had to take priority in my life. I told Marlena that I wanted to give her a massage, too. I wanted to touch her.

I massaged Marlena's neck for a few minutes. The smell of her hair seeped into me. I did not think. Thinking was done. Her body radiated warmth. I had no doubts. I stood by the side of the table, put my left hand behind her neck, caressed her cheek with my right hand, bent over and gave her a warm and lingering kiss. She responded for a fraction of a significant moment before she turned away and got off the table.

She was disturbed. I had violated a big taboo. When you are giving a massage, you never are to take advantage of someone's trust and vulnerability. But I had.

She left the house. The next day, she called and told me that I was not to kiss her because she was married. I agreed. I thought about it a lot after she called. I did not want to cause Marlena any distress.

ONCE I KISSED HER, ONCE SHE RESPONDED FOR A SLIVER OF A second, once she told me not to kiss her but a few days later agreed to meet me for dinner, then I knew my way.

What had brought me this confidence? Me, a disfigured, middle-aged man without a steady job, no savings, a life built on denial, with many foolish and stupid life choices under my belt? What gave me the confidence to go for Marlena, a married woman? Married for many years, in an apparently stable marriage to a fine, solid, financially well-off man? With a home in the redwood trees? With a hot tub? Marlena never ever spoke ill of her husband, Larry, not once, not even by implication.

It all came together then. The months visiting David, with his death helping me focus on life and love. The months working together with Marlena, doing massage for ill and dying patients at CPMC. I was no longer turning to alcohol to blunt and cover my true self. Yes, my habits of denial helped give me courage too. But it was also touch—the touch built trust at a time in my life when I had learned not to trust words. I stopped trying to live up to ideals so much; I was drawn into my own body, just as it was. The trust that was engendered in Marlena by touch also turned out to be trust in myself.

And, to be fair, Marlena seduced me. She seduced me quietly, not only by nurturing touch but also by her persistence, by seeing who I was, by valuing me, by taking that second and third and fourth long look. I had experienced the language of love. Touch had bypassed my consciousness and worked on the deepest cellular level. My soul had waited years for this time.

After our dinner date, I asked Marlena to take a walk. Right across the street, right across Mission, up the western side of Bernal Hill and around to the north side. Below us was San Francisco at the end of a glorious summer day. The eastern half of the city glowed gold under a blue

California sky. Summer fog wrapped itself over Twin Peaks in a slow, roiling, gray tsunami and the wind off the ocean blew streaky fog fingers toward Berkeley and Oakland, where the late sun turned hundreds of windows into diamonds.

And there it was, the first real kiss, the one that sealed the deal, the kiss of no return.

Marlena needed time to think.

I worried what I was doing was wrong. Some of my friends encouraged me, others were wary.

My friend Paula taught an adult education class on dealing with divorce. She made it clear to me that women nearing the end of their marriages often found a sympathetic man to help and encourage them. And that 85 percent of the time, these relationships ended soon after the marriage ended.

I talked about Marlena with Sharon, my spiritual advisor. I thought that Sharon would disapprove because Marlena was married. But she was supportive. She suggested I might consider judging my relationship with Marlena by what was happening outside of the relationship. Was I growing stronger? Was Marlena? What was happening in other parts of our lives? The answers were clear. Marlena was building her massage practice as she had hoped. I had quit my job as a programmer analyst and started a part-time massage practice while attending City College of San Francisco. We loved our volunteer work building the massage program at Pacific Presbyterian Medical Center. We were thriving.

WE HAD KNOWN EACH OTHER FOR NINE MONTHS. WE BECAME lovers on Day Street, with the warmth of solstice sun and the summer breeze bringing the aroma of jasmine through the window full force into the bedroom. The next morning, I sat down at the kitchen table and wrote Marlena a letter asking her to get a divorce and marry me. I told her that I understood that leaving Larry would be difficult.

She told me she would need a long time to think. And she had to get ready to talk honestly with Larry.

AT ONE POINT, MARLENA ASKED ME TO STOP SEEING OTHER women. I thought it was quite unfair. She was married to Larry! I examined my actions again and again. Every time I had doubts, I talked about it. Why am I in a relationship with a married woman? A monogamous relationship with a woman who was married to someone else was not high on my list of desirable characteristics in a relationship. Not on my list at all, as a matter of fact. What right did she have to be jealous?

But of course it was flattering too.

I thought about it. I thought about it for months. It was not an instantaneous choice, not at all. Her marriage to Larry was ending, and in that ending, Marlena was honest and straightforward with Larry and with me. I had promised Marlena patience and support in that process. Yes, she was married, but every time she was with me, she was totally present.

At times I wished that Larry were more of a jerk, but he wasn't, and Marlena did not see him that way. The process of ending her marriage took longer than I thought it should, but I saw too that the respect that Marlena gave to Larry and to their relationship, even as it was ending, was a quality that she would also bring to our relationship.

So I agreed to be monogamous with a married woman.

I was sitting in the Planetree Library at California Pacific Medical Center, studying anatomy. One of the librarians came up to me as I was bent over my books. She said, "I thought you might be interested in this," and set in front of me a booklet entitled *The Let's Face It Resource Guide for People with Facial Difference.* She quickly walked away. I was angry and embarrassed. I brought the booklet home and showed it to Marlena. I told her, "I want nothing to do with this."

Later Marlena and I were having dinner. It occurred to me that she might be interested in finding out what happened to my face. So I asked her if she wanted to know. She smiled and said, "I thought you'd never ask." I began to talk in unfamiliar ways about who I was. My heart spoke more than my head. I did not feel like this was a big breakthrough for me; it just felt natural and right.

The skin is the most superficial of all the human organs, but it was through the skin that I was first touched deeply. It started with skin and grew more and more into words, into my whole life.

DEEP INTO OUR MARRIAGE, IT IS A SUNDAY MORNING. MARlena has her head covered with the blanket, as usual. I reach over her and open the shade, revealing the bay laurel over Mill Creek. A little bit of sun comes through cracks in the leafy overhead of the creek bed. One of the prisms catches a ray and arranges rainbows on the wall over the head board. It is a chilly winter day, below freezing. The creek is running clear after the last few days of heavy rain.

I gaze around the room. The ficus is in winter mode, with no new growth, the leaves covered with dust from the heating system. I ponder bringing in cotton pads and rubbing alcohol and instituting a schedule of cleaning the leaves. Marlena loves the ficus; she rescued it when it was about to be thrown out by a neighbor and has restored it to good health.

On the windowsill, six hyacinth bulbs have taken good

root in their forcing vases. Each of them has a strong bud coming up. I think that they will be blooming within ten days, on my birthday.

My feet are cold. I tuck them up under Marlena's thighs. My right arm is chilly because it is outside the blanket. There is a delicious disparity between the parts of me connected to Marlena's metabolic furnace and the chilly parts of me. I wonder why it feels so good.

My right hand reaches over and rubs Marlena's head, using all four fingers for maximum effect. She murmurs with delight and snuggles closer. I bend my head over and smell her hair. I find tightness on either side of her cervical spine and work it a bit. I have not noticed that area before.

Looking around the room, looking out at the creek and the peeks of sun through the trees; smelling the bay laurel and the creek and Marlena's familiar morning breath; soaking up her warmth, the sense of needing to strive slips away. The day ahead no longer feels like a weight on my chest. I grow slightly dizzy with delight; my respiration and pulse slow. In her presence, in her warmth, in the laying on of hands, there is a sufficiency, a plenitude of touch.

EIGHT

UNCONDITIONAL LOVE HAS ITS CONDITIONS

In the Church of 80% Sincerity we believe in unconditional love. But we realize that it has a shelf life of about five to ten seconds.

This has practical ramifications. For example, we understand that you can't just say to a man, "I love you." That terrifies him. But if you understand the true nature of unconditional love, you can say, "Sweetheart, I have these feelings of love for you that last about eight seconds." This is something a man can deal with—a nice neat package of quantified emotions. Then he will start wondering: "Why only eight seconds?" Then you can up the ante. "Honey, I know I will love you till the end . . . of dinner."

*　*　*

FOR A LONG TIME, I BELIEVED THAT NO ONE COULD EVER LOVE someone as grotesque and disfigured as myself. With that belief in place inside me, I had difficulty recognizing love, let alone taking it in. The barriers to love were most always of my own construction. Unconditional love is scary, because we think we do not deserve it.

The key to recognizing and receiving unconditional love is to be open to it without conditions. It is hard because we all carry around a list of reasons why we are unloveable: teeth not white enough, inferior vehicle, being a sinner, too old, not enough money, no sense of humor, inadequate body hair, habit of sort of picking nose, snoring, habit of saying inappropriate things, being a bad girl or boy. Think of the things that come to mind when you wake up at three a.m.

The true composition of love: 20 percent feelings, 80 percent action. Feelings of love are great when they are present, and they can inspire us to loving action, but they do come and go.

I had to learn slowly to open the door just a crack to let love in, maybe just a few seconds at a time. We all do.

GROWING UP, I DO NOT RECALL MY FATHER EVER TELLING ME that he loved me. But he showed me how to:

- Tuck my chin down behind my left shoulder and lead with my left when boxing;

- Receive a handoff from a quarterback in order to avoid fumbling;

- Get in front of a ground ball so it would bounce off me if I did not catch it;

- Box out other rebounders in basketball.

My father showed me how to believe in my own body—that was how he told me he loved me. He held a vision of what I could be physically, not judging me by limitations, and with that encouragement I could grow into that vision.

SISTER FRIEDA TAUGHT SEVENTH GRADE. SHE SCARED ME when she bent over my desk with her voluminous black robes and the white thing around her face and the black thing over her head like a shawl, with her eyes that seemed too large through her wire-rimmed glasses and her funny breath and the dots on her nose that my mother had to explain were just enlarged pores. But she encouraged me. Without my permission, she had signed me up for the Lake County spelling bee sponsored by the Hammond *Times.* I would never have done that on my own.

I spelled picnicking without the *k* and finished in second place. I was given a Benrus watch, but it was for failure. I had failed my parents, Our Lady of Grace School, my classmates and Sister Frieda.

After the bee, my parents and I drove home. We took an unfamiliar turn and my mother explained we were going to visit the convent. I did not really know what a convent was; my general impression was that the nuns were kept in some sort of storage area and only let out to teach us. I did not want to reveal my failure to Sister Frieda.

We rang the doorbell. Sister Frieda came into the foyer and was clearly happy to see us. She raised a questioning eyebrow and I burst into tears. "Second," I muttered. Sister Frieda threw her head back and laughed. She stepped toward me, beaming. I stood rooted and miserable. She kept coming, and then she hugged me. I kept my arms by my side and disappeared into yards of black cloth and the smell of Cashmere Bouquet soap. A nun hugged me. In that action that seemed so improbable and shocking to me, in her moment of joy and pleasure at what she saw as my success, in her willingness to be spontaneous and, in my mind, most un-nun-like, I caught a glimpse of unconditional love. She gave me the gift of faith in me before I had faith in myself.

*　*　*

ONE NIGHT DURING THE SUMMER I WAS FIFTEEN, I ARRIVED home a little after ten-thirty. Entering the kitchen through the back door, I called out, "Home!" and heard my mother respond, "Dave, bring me the salami and cheese." I fixed a plate of thin-sliced hard salami, Swiss cheese and Ritz crackers and brought it into the dining room.

My mother was at her accustomed spot at the table, squatting peasant style on the chair as she always did, watching Johnny Carson finish his monologue. She wore a white flannel nightgown, and over that a red cotton robe, washed many times, soft and worn. My father had gone to bed.

She chuckled at the TV. Her chuckle turned into a long minute of emphysemic coughing. She sipped her beer to quell the coughing, and then tilted her head forward, peering over her glasses, listening to who Johnny's guests would be.

I offered her the salami and cheese during a commercial. She took a couple of the crackers and placed them in a row on a tissue in front of her. We sat and watched Johnny do his swami thing for a while.

Mom turned and asked, "How are you, Dave?" I knew it wasn't important what we talked about. She was there to listen, to check in, and to encourage. "Dave, you could be anything you want to be because you are so smart. You know, Dave, you are so creative, you would be a good designer."

Mom was under the influence of the Stroh's beer, but I did

not understand that then, and even now, when I do understand, it still doesn't make a whole lot of difference.

Because I believed her. I never knew what a designer did, exactly, but Mom said it so often and with such conviction that I totally believed her.

I WAS A LITTLE NERVOUS ABOUT JON WHEN I FIRST MET HIM. He was twenty-one, very young-looking, slim, with a cavalier's flowing curls. A Jewish-hippie hairdo. He was very warm-hearted and everyone seemed to like him. And he was gay.

I had had gay friends before. Or, I should say, I knew gay people. But I had not been a friend. Seemed like strange territory. In the seminary, the priests told us, "If another boy puts his arm around you, tell him 'take a powder, Elsie.'" That was the limit of my understanding of homosexuality.

Jon was different. I could tell he was interested in me, but it wasn't a sexual thing. He just liked me. I did not understand that at first.

My first wife, Joan, and I had been cofounders of the cooperative childcare center located at Bethany Methodist Church in San Francisco. Jon lived in the parsonage next door and volunteered at the center.

He started inviting me to his room. I declined at first, and then went sort of reluctantly. I had never been invited into a gay man's bedroom before. We sat. I looked out the window at the people coming in and out of Angel's Market on the corner of Twenty-sixth and Sanchez.

"So, Dave, how did the day go today?"

"Oh, good. Good."

"What do you mean?"

"Oh, we went to Finnila's Family Spa with the kids. You know, that is always good. They love to play in the water."

"I love Finnila's."

"Yeah, me too. Yeah."

"Anything else happen?"

"Oh, Douglas Park. Adam got lost but he was just digging behind the restrooms."

"But, you know, how did the day go for you?"

"Well, like I said. Lunch was good, lunch was good."

"But I mean, how did the day go for you?"

"Well, it was good, I guess. What do you mean? Nothing bad happened."

"I mean, how did you feel about what happened?"

"How did I what? I just told you, I thought."

He sighed. "Dave, I am interested in your feelings, in you as a person, not just the kids."

I fidgeted in my chair. His words alarmed me, not because of any sexual charge, but because of the intimacy. Revealing my feelings to another person, another man, a gay man—was new and scary. The whole concept of feelings as an actual topic of conversation was weird. Jon kept at it and kept at it, helping me to explore my feelings, to even acknowledge that they existed. It was a gift.

In 2001 I had sclerotherapy to downsize swollen veins in my throat, tongue and soft palate. The treatment included a tracheotomy because there was concern that my airway would be too blocked for me to breathe when I got out of surgery. I was scheduled to stay in the Intensive Care Unit for up to ten days, but after only three, I was downgraded from the seven thousand dollars per day ICU to an ordinary two thousand dollars per day hospital room. I did not receive as much attention as I did in the ICU, but Room L1422 had TV and a view that included the east end of Golden Gate Park as well as downtown San Francisco. It was all very beautiful in the December rain.

I was still "tube city" and I felt bludgeoned. But I had graduated from the ICU. I lay there with a dim sense of having survived. My friend Kathleena was giving me a foot rub. My friend Ginger was doing Feldenkrais bodywork on my left shoulder. My dear daughter, Amy, was sitting at the bedside, her hand resting on my knee. She began to read aloud the "Morning Prayers" that she and Marlena helped me to write before I went into the hospital.

"I let go and trust in God and my friends. I am supported by prayers and love from all over the world." Amy paused, and then repeated that sentence.

Her voice shook me. For all the times I have been in the hospital, I have tried to be a good boy, a good patient, enduring whatever had to be done, impressing the doctors with my spirit and, hopefully, my immune system. I had to survive.

But now, Amy's voice eased me into a new place as I was held by Kathleena and Ginger. I began to let go as words and touch coursed through me.

Amy continued. She read each line carefully and slowly.

"My life force and immune system are strong. I accept my treatment well. There is just enough sclerosing and swelling for proper healing, no more, no less. Those who care for me are fully present and operating at their highest skill level."

I began to weep, wheezing through the trach, then sobbed and sobbed for twenty minutes, the most I have ever cried at one time in my entire life. In that one overwhelming moment of unconditional love, what I had thought was my stoic strength slipped away.

YES, THERE ARE CONDITIONS ON UNCONDITIONAL LOVE. IT has its limitations in duration and it comes in forms that are not always recognizable and sometimes scary and often small and often strange.

Before we learn about love, we usually do not know what it is when we receive it. I did not know how much my father loved me until well after he died. Or how much I loved him. I did not know what Jon was giving me. Or Sister Frieda. Or my mother.

We build channels and dikes and levees to keep love from flooding us, because it is so unbelievable that we could be so loved. But it is still unconditional love, it is still there—we have to open ourselves to make it real.

It is okay to take it in slowly. That, I think, is part of the human condition. We do the best we can according to our circumstances.

Or maybe it's not a flood. Maybe it's more like this: It comes in bits and pieces, fragments and shards. These become building blocks that we can use to form our own wholeness and character.

Now I look back and see so many times, so many other ways and times that I was loved.

I always felt love from Joe Montana and the San Francisco 49ers. They were always trying their best for me. Even if they lost, they tried hard.

The Birthmark and Vascular Anomalies Center at the University of California at San Francisco Medical Center.

My nana. When I stayed with her as a child, she'd sing to me: "Good morning, merry sunshine. How did you wake so soon? You scared the little stars away and shined away the moon." I knew it was a song for babies. But Nana loved it. And so did I. Then she would say, "Aren't you the one? Aren't you the one?" Or "Aren't you looking good this morning?" The joy she felt at seeing me was so manifest that I loved to stand still and let it wash over me.

Dr. Christopher Dowd, who performed sclerotherapy on my throat and soft palate and tongue. Before the procedure he talked with me for almost two hours in his office.

The nurses in the ICU. (But that may have been the morphine.)

When I first met Marlena and then fell in love with her, I was sure that Sharon, my spiritual advisor at that time, would judge me as immoral. Instead she saw me as a human being trying to be true to my own heart and conscience at the same time.

Some months after Joan and I split up, I asked my daughter what she would think if I had a girlfriend. Amy said, "Fine, Dad, as long as she likes kids and pays her share of the rent."

My friend Art came down from Milwaukee to visit me after our freshman year at Saint Lawrence Seminary. I had decided to be ashamed of my parents. I was not really ashamed of them; I somehow thought it was cool. I met Art at the South Shore station in Hammond and on the bus to

Highland, I began apologizing for how foolish and stupid my parents were. Art grabbed my shirt and said, "Don't ever talk that way about your parents." And I never did after that.

Like a child constantly rebuilding the same Lego structure day after day, I have to use these blocks, these seconds and moments of unconditional love from throughout my life, every day, to remember that I am loved. It still slips away; the fears come back. Instead of greeting them, I reach for my memories of the love I have received throughout my life, the bits and pieces of affection and regard, my blocks. They are solid under my fingertips. The fears take flight.

NINE

PITILESS

"PISS ON PITY" IS A POPULAR SLOGAN AMONG disability rights activists. It means: Don't pity us because of our perceived disabilities. You have no right to judge us. You have no idea what our lives are like.

THE FIRST TIME MARLENA TOLD THE STORY OF when she met me and how she came to love me, it was before an audience made up of parents of children with Nager Syndrome and Miller Syndrome—children who are often born without mandibles, without eyelids, with flipper limbs, among other conditions. Marlena ended the story of coming to love someone with a facial difference by saying, "I think I saw David's soul."

I looked out at the parents and saw them entranced. They knew exactly what Marlena was talking about because they had seen the souls of their own children. They were silent for several long moments, then began applauding slowly, it seemed out of a sense of propriety. Then a woman stood up and began speaking. Her name was Mary; she was a heavyset doula from the Canadian prairies. She told of being present at the birth of Patrick, who came into the world with deficiencies severe enough that he lived only twenty minutes after emerging from the womb. Patrick spent those twenty minutes being held and cherished by his mother.

Mary said, "I realized, who am I, who am I to feel sad for Patrick? Who am I to judge his life? All of us, our lives, however long we live, they are all a blink in the life of the universe, of God's eternal love. Here, Patrick spent his whole lifetime being nurtured and loved and held. What a happy, full life he led."

IT IS ADULTS RATHER THAN CHILDREN WHO PITY ME. Occasionally I will hear something from this litany:

"Oh, my God! What happened to your face?"

"You know, if I looked like you, I don't think I could go outside."

"You have so much courage. If I had a face like that, I really think I would consider killing myself."

"You must have had a terrible life."

"You know, God loves you even if other people don't."

"I feel so very sorry for you."

I say, "Thank you." I try to acknowledge the goodness of their intentions, their kindness in trying to reach out and comfort me. I try not to pity them.

Understand that comments like these are rare. Mostly, adults are satisfied with a glance held a bit longer. Or they avert their faces.

Children, however, don't waste too much time on pity. Once they get over any shyness, they get right to the point:

"You are smiling too much."

"What happened to your mouth?"

"What happened to your chin?"

"Where did your chin go?"

"What is that stuff on the side of your face?"

"Why is your eye too big?"

"Does your face hurt?"

Four- and five-year-olds are interested in monsters, and when someone like me appears outside of one of their storybooks, they can be startled.

* * *

A MOMENT AGO DEREK HAD BEEN WHINING AT HIS MOTHER, working toward obtaining one of the large chocolate chip cookies that he had spotted on display on the coffeehouse counter. "Wouldn't you rather have a bagel, Derek? A cinnamon bagel? The kind you like?" But abruptly he is not paying attention to the cookie. He has seen me. The whiny face disappears instantaneously. (I ought to hire out my services with the slogan "Quasimodo Child Distracters. Mood Changes Guaranteed.") Derek's eyes widen. His mouth opens. He backs up half a step, never taking me out of his sight. He puts a knuckle in his mouth while he takes a moment to regard me with alarm. He is wondering if I am a monster. But monsters live under the bed or in the closet or in the bushes, not in the place where his mother gets coffee.

He looks at his mother. She has a look that is half relief, half here-comes-a-big-faux-pas. "Honey, come and sit." But Derek has started circling me in a six-foot radius. He is pretty sure I am not a monster but he is not sure if I am real. Only my dermatologist examines me so closely. He isn't just checking out my face. He looks to see what is on the table, he looks at my briefcase. He looks for monster accoutrements. I look up and give him a small smile. He gives a little wave. He stops every forty-five degrees to take a mental photo. Do I look like maybe SpongeBob Squarepants? Or somebody from *Sesame Street*?

Somewhere in his brain, in his imagination, he is forming a picture, he is forming a way of understanding people who are different, whose faces are not symmetrical.

I WAS VERY NERVOUS THE FIRST TIME MARLENA AND I PRE-sented "Love at Second Sight" at a middle school. But the students were rapt right from the opening moment, when I said "I want you to stare at my face today." They loved the fact that we talked frankly about appearance and acceptability—the two things they cared about the most in life. The kids gave us a standing ovation, and I was bubbling.

An earnest young man came up to me afterward. He said, "Wow, that was so cool. You were great. You are a great actor." I preened for a couple seconds and then he continued, "Yeah, you could be one of those weird creatures on *Star Trek.*"

AFTER A SHOW IN SECHELT, BRITISH COLUMBIA, I DID A question-and-answer session. The first person to raise his hand was a young teenager named Dennis. I later found out that he had multiple disabilities, mostly intellectual and emo-tional, that he had been often in trouble with the law.

Dennis stood up and said nothing for ten or fifteen sec-onds, looking up, then down, apparently searching for words.

Then he said, "Up until tonight, all my heroes were not like me. They wore costumes, they were superheroes. Now that I have met you, I have a hero who is like me."

That was the best compliment I've ever received after performing.

YOUNG PEOPLE APPROACH ME ON THE STREET AND SAY THAT they remember when I came to their school and that it was the best assembly they ever had. They can never tell me what exactly they remember, or what was good about it, but they do remember that it was cool and I was cool.

I always want to hear more than that, but I know that all we really remember accurately about our personal experiences is our feelings. We make up a story from the bits and pieces, the shards of what we think are facts, the supposed "truth" of the story. What we are doing is constructing a story that makes sense of our feelings at the time it happened (as well as our present-day feelings).

It doesn't seem to make much difference to them what I had to say. That doesn't stick. But the fact that I was there has great significance.

PEOPLE DO STARE. PEOPLE DO ASK WHAT HAPPENED TO MY face. I don't always give that nice educational answer. Sometimes I'm grouchy. I feel like saying: "You've heard of a bad hair day. Well, I am having a bad face day." I have never actually done this—but I have been tempted to tell a child who is pestering and obnoxious, "No, son, my face doesn't hurt. . . . Well, my face is like this because when I was a little boy like you, I touched my wee-wee."

FOR MANY YEARS I AVOIDED SITUATIONS WHERE I COULD BE stared at. I interpreted staring as hostile and prejudicial. Now, mainly from being around the honesty of children, I've learned some incredibly important life lessons.

They need a few minutes to get used to me, and will take the time to do so unless their parents intervene out of concern that the child is not being courteous. Now I see that it is normal, that everyone needs a little time to get used to somebody unusual in appearance. I know I do.

So I get it. That first ten minutes is not prejudice. It is adjustment time. Free time. Staring is not necessarily pleasant, but it is not hostile. It's okay.

I used to try to stare back, to embarrass starers on the bus, the subway, the airport, the mall. Now I am more at peace. I realize that I am on earth with a disfigured face, with a strong stage presence and sense of humor. I am inspiring. So be it.

* * *

From interactions with children I began to understand that my appearance can stir four levels of fear in people who first encounter me.

One is at the level of protocol, of social niceties. How should I behave with this person who looks so different? Am I going to do something wrong or offensive?

Second is the fear of contagion, that there is a disease to be transmitted.

Third, there is a fear of violence, a fear engendered by all of the movies and fairy tales portraying the facially disfigured carrying chainsaws as casually as normal people have cell phones. This is the source of children fearing us as monsters.

The fourth fear, the root fear, is the fear inside, that they are disfigured in some way externally or internally, in some way unacceptable and unloveable to family, village, species, perhaps even to God.

I trigger that fear, and at a spiritual level it's also a fear of an uncaring God who is capable of creating people who are so deeply flawed that they are not in God's image and hence irredeemable. And that's what I symbolize.

And that is what pity covers up.

I deal with stares, comments and occasional cruelties every time I walk out my front door. It is not the fact of my disfigurement that wears on my psyche. It is the fear and self-doubt of others, their very human concern about their own social acceptability, their worry about being unloveable and abandoned, which they project onto me.

IT IS THE PITILESS CHILDREN WHO APPROACH WITH HONEST fear and wonderment who offer the best opportunities for me. The more I am able to be patient with them, to wait until they adjust to my appearance and see the light in my eyes, the more I relax and be myself, then I see them relax and smile and feel joy at having gotten to know me.

I want children to remember that it is good to be honest, good to approach someone who looks different, good to find out what they are really like.

I SQUATTED DOWN IN FRONT OF DEREK. "DEREK, WERE YOU wondering what happened to my face?" He nodded. "Well, you know that everybody looks different. And this is just the way I look. My face doesn't hurt. I look different, but I am just a regular person. My name is David."

TEN

FAITH
AT
RANDOM

I HAVE HEARD THAT GOD EXISTS. BUT IN THE interest of full disclosure, I am informing you that I have never actually met him.

When I was a young child, I believed in God because I was told to. Just like I believed in the story of the girl who got a needle pushed through her thumbnail because she played with the sewing machine when her grandmother told her not to. It actually was a little easier to believe in the little girl's story because I could see the sewing machine needle flashing up and down when my grandmother sewed.

Saint Thomas—Doubting Thomas—did not believe that Jesus had risen from the dead. The other apostles told him they had seen him, but he said, "Unless I can put my hand in his wound, I do not believe." And of course Jesus showed up, teased Thomas a bit, and then forgave him. Jesus ended by saying, "Blessed are those who have not seen, but have yet believed."

Me, I would have been right there with Saint Thomas. I live in California. I would have thought, oh, this is some New Age bullshit. Those apostles paid big money for a Tony Robbins resurrection workshop and they all bought into it.

The nuns told us that God was everywhere. I immediately wondered if God was in the toilet and could see my butt. I had sense enough not to ask that question out loud but, as you know, God knew my innermost thoughts.

Since then I have had contact with God only through intermediaries: trees, flowers, friends and the like. Perhaps the toilet thing offended him.

I have not been able to reach God by the standard means like prayer and meditation. He does not answer.

You'd think that he would stay in better contact. He hasn't written in almost two thousand years. At least I am told he hasn't written. I check the mailbox from time to time.

It's difficult for me to imagine what God is like. I can fantasize that I am a sixty-three-year-old, five-foot-five-inch tall professional basketball player. I can fantasize having a relationship with Hillary Clinton. I can imagine what I will do when I win the Super Lotto. But somehow I can't work up a good God fantasy.

Faith always seemed like an intellectual cosmic choice. But it is not. Faith comes through life experience. It is not in the head; it is in the heart. Faith is an experience, not dogma imposed from above. It is the recognition of the quality of your own experience, moving from head to heart.

Faith comes as an IV drip, not a drenching, not a waterfall.

Willpower will get you started, will get you to take the risk that gives you the experience upon which faith is based.

I have faith because I believe in nothing. I clear it all out of my head. In my head I believe in nothing. That leaves the route to my heart open. In my heart I believe in everything and everyone.

To be a performer, I had to have faith in my ability. I didn't at first. I had willpower and ambition. But I did have faith in my friends who had faith in me. I have it because people have mirrored it back to me. I have built faith through the experience of friends.

The nuns told us that faith is a gift. I understand that to mean that it is not individual, but formed in relationship with others, with nature, with environment.

Faith is a life work, a choice made daily. Faith eats fear for lunch, but someone has to kill the fear and cook it.

I believe I am on earth with a noticeable facial disfigurement, that I have great stage presence, creativity and humor. I believe that I can bring courage, inspiration and laughter to others. I believe I can best do that by being myself as much as possible. In this, I have faith.

Acknowledgments

I gratefully acknowledge:

My editor, Meg Leder, who saw what this book could be and brought it to birth, at all times with wisdom and a generous spirit; John Duff, Craig Burke, Patrick Nolan and the rest of the encouraging Penguin team.

Anne Lamott, inexorably inspiring in person and in print. She told me I had to write this book. So I did. Bird by bird.

My agent, Robyn Stecher, an openhearted warrior and a dear friend.

My constant creative allies Jo Anne Smith and Terri Tate.

My writing partners, who cast creative and critical eyes on my work: Karin Bergen, Persimmon Blackbridge, Merijane Block, Zoe Borkowski, Joanie Chapman, Dennis DeBiase, Neshama Franklin, Kathleena Gorga, Robin Jacobson, Kate Jones, Rosa Kochur, Stephanie Moore, Tina Osinski, Kenn Rabin, Marje Umezuki, Abby Wasserman, Carol Howard Wooton and the Thursday group at O'Hanlon Center for the Arts.

Those who laid the groundwork for this book by helping me find my creative voice in my middle years:

Those who came before me, especially Nana, who lit the spark inside me, and Mom, who made me believe I could do anything.

My sisters and brothers, Craig, Kathleen, Patrick, Kevin, Michael, Teresa: the garden where my sense of humor grew.

Art Noble, for believing in me as a writer since we were both thirteen years old.

Lee Glickstein, for helping me discover my performing creativity.

San Francisco's nurturing theater community, especially Sarah Corr, Corey Fischer, Daniel Hoffman, Kenn Watt, The Magic Theatre and A Travelling Jewish Theatre.

My colleagues in disability culture around the world. With a special thanks to Cheryl Marie Wade, a dear and deliciously wicked mentor. Lisa Bufano, Jeanne Calvit, Vickie Cammack, Gretchen Case, Linda Chernoff, Joe Coughlin, Michelle Decottignies, Char Curtiss, Tony Doyle, Nicole Dunbar, Eufemia Fantetti, Jim Ferris, Joanna Finch, Max Fomitchev, Mat Fraser, Marc Goldman, Ruth Gould, Bob Guter, Anita Hollander, Gary Karp, John Killacky, Petra Kuppers, Riva Lehrer, Deborah Lewis, Simi Linton, Lawrence Carter Long, Neil Marcus, Victoria Maxwell, David Mitchell, Julie McNamara, Kathy Martinez, Judy Norbury, Philip Patston, Olivia Raynor, Leslie Roman, Denise Roza, Joel Rutledge, Carrie Sandahl, Alan Shain, Sima Elizabeth Shefrin, Betty Siegel, Sharon Snyder, Spirit Synott, VSA Arts, Pamela Walker, Gail Williamson, Sharon Wolfe, Liane Yasumoto and Gwennan Young.

All the creative crew associated with *Shameless: The ART*

of Disability, especially mother duck/director Bonnie Klein and Persimmon Blackbridge, Catherine Frazee and Geoff McMurchy.

The storytellers: Carol LaDue, Amy Metzenbaum, Kay Pepitone, Lynn Rogers, Janet Ryvlin, Susan Amanda Schratter, Evangeline Welch, Carol Howard Wooton and Warren Wooton.

People who kept my body and spirit alive: Sharon Anderson, Ken Barnes, Jeannie Battagin, Barbara Besser, Chris Burns, Susan Christy, Christian Coon, Chris Dowd, Tedi Dunn, Daniel Frank, Ilona Frieden, Joan Gardner, David Garfinkel, Larry Haimovitch, Carie Harris, Jon Herzstam, Karen Huckabay, Paula Horowitz, Susan Hughes, Laura Ingram, Nancy Kelly, David Kleinberg, Jonathan Levy, Ginger McLeod, John Malloy, Virginia Mason, Jeri Pearson, David Pitonyak, Jeri Praul, Allison Rennie, Gail Stein, Thad Tecza, Gary Titus and Marian Williams.

Friends who understand facial difference: American Cleft Palate-Craniofacial Association, Francine Blei, Khrista Boylan, Children's Craniofacial Association, Craniofacial Association, Lindsay Fisher, FACES, Patricia Fontaine, Forward Face, Rickey Gill, Mike Grundmann, Margaret Hogan, Matt Joffe, Karen LeClair, Frances Cooke MacGregor, Joseph McCarthy, Debby Oliver, Phoenix Society, Anna Pileggi, David Reisberg, Lorna Renooy, Betsy Wilson, Ginny Wood, Tanya Workman and Gail Zimmerman.

Finally, a constant source of love, laughter and intense light in my life, my daughter, Amy, with her fantastic husband, Steve Mascari, and son, Jason.

About the Author

David Roche was born in Hammond, Indiana, the eldest of seven children. His sixteen years of Roman Catholic education included four years studying to be a priest at Saint Lawrence Seminary in Wisconsin. David graduated magna cum laude from Saint Joseph's College with a BA in philosophy. As a motivational speaker and humorist, he has appeared throughout the United States, including at the Clinton White House, as well as in Canada, England, Russia, New Zealand and Australia. *The Church of 80% Sincerity* is his first book and is based on his signature one-man show of the same title. He and his wife, Marlena Blavin, live on the Sunshine Coast of British Columbia and in Marin County, California.